Workout
Skills Review & Practice

Reading Grade 3

Triumph Learning®

Workout, Reading, Grade 3
262NA
ISBN-10: 1-60471-113-2
ISBN-13: 978-1-60471-113-4

Cover Image: © Ralph Voltz/Deborah Wolfe Ltd.; © Rubberball/Jupiterimages;
© Imagesource/Photolibrary; © Creatas/Photolibrary.

Triumph Learning® 136 Madison Avenue, 7th Floor, New York, NY 10016
Kevin McAliley, President and Chief Executive Officer

Printed in the United States of America.

10 9 8 7 6 5 4

Dear Student,

Are you a reading champion?

You will be when you use

Workout!

Getting in shape is easy.

Just complete the lessons inside.

So, on your mark, get set—Work Out!

This book belongs to _____

Table of Contents

Unit 1: Reading for Information

Unit 2: Reading Literature

Unit 3: Writing, Editing, Mechanics

LESSON 1 Reference Books

WORDS TO KNOW **Reference books** help you find information and answer questions. A **dictionary** tells you what words mean. A **thesaurus** tells you words you can use in place of other words. An **atlas** contains maps. **Encyclopedias** and the **Internet** give information on many topics.

Review It!

Read these sentences. Use the Hint to help you figure out which reference source you should use.

You need to write a report about the planets in our solar system. Should you start your research with a dictionary or an encyclopedia?

Hint An encyclopedia is a set of books that give general information about many topics. A dictionary only defines terms, such as planet.

Try It!

Read this passage. As you read, underline circle the names of reference sources that provide information.

1. Matt is writing a report about bats. He knows there are many kinds of
2. bats. He wants to choose one or two to write about. Matt begins his
3. library research. First he looks on the Internet. He types "bats" into the
4. online search engine. Many articles pop up. Matt writes down websites
5. that he thinks will be helpful and that he wants to come back to later.
6. Then he looks for the encyclopedias. He takes a volume from the shelf
7. and finds his topic. Reading the article helps him decide that he will write
8. about fruit bats and horseshoe bats.

Now, use the passage to answer the questions on the following page.

1. In line 5, how would Matt choose a website to use?

    A. He finds a website all about bats.

    B. He finds a site with lots of bat jokes.

    C. He finds a site created a long time ago.

    D. He finds a site with a nice name.

2. On the bat website, how will Matt find out what information it has?

    A. He will call the person who made the site.

    B. He will ask his teacher.

    C. He will click on different links.

    D. He will ask his father for help.

3. Matt is looking for information about bats. Which volume of the encyclopedia should he look in?

    A. Volume I: A–Be   **C.** Volume III: Ch–D

    B. Volume II: Bf–Ce   **D.** Volume IV: E–Fe

    > **3.**
    > What are the first two letters of the word *bat?*

4. Matt decides to write about fruit bats. Which section of the encyclopedia article should he read?

    A. "Where Bats Live"   **C.** "What Bats Eat"

    B. "Kinds of Bats"   **D.** "How Bats Fly"

    > **4.**
    > Which sources would you definitely not use?

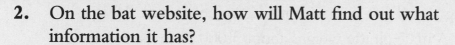

5. You have a set of encyclopedias. Each volume covers one letter of the alphabet. Volume 1 includes all the A topics. Volume 2 includes all the B topics. In which volume would you find information about frogs? Give the letter and the number.

    > **5.**
    > What letter of the alphabet does *frog* start with?

    _____

    _____

On Your Own!

Read this part of Ana's report about giraffes. Answer the questions that follow it.

Giraffes live in Africa. They are the tallest land animals. A full-grown male giraffe can be up to 18 feet tall. A giraffe's neck is about six feet long. Its legs are about six feet long, too. What holds up those long legs? A giraffe has really big feet. Each one is about 12 inches across. All that size weighs a lot, too. A male giraffe weighs about 3,000 pounds. A female weighs about 1,500 pounds.

It takes a lot of food to keep a big animal going. A giraffe can eat up to 75 pounds of food every day. Giraffes eat leaves. Their favorites are from the thorny acacia tree. The thorns don't bother the giraffes as they eat. They use their really long tongues to reach around most of the thorns. A giraffe's tongue is about 18 inches long!

Because giraffes are so big, they do not hide from predators. They are hunted by lions and crocodiles. These predators try to grab giraffes when they are bent over a watering hole. But a giraffe can defend itself with its powerful kick. Giraffes can also run quickly to escape predators.

1. In which encyclopedia volume did Ana look to find information for her report?

   A. Volume 1: A
   B. Volume 4: Cr-Cz
   C. Volume 6: F-G
   D. Volume 12: O-P

2. At the beginning of an article about giraffes, Ana will **probably** find

   A. general information about giraffes
   B. information about mammals
   C. information about what giraffes eat
   D. information about Africa

3. Ana has found a website about Africa to use for background information. Which link should she click to get recent population figures?

   A. "Africa's Landscape"

   B. "Africa's History"

   C. "Africa's Economy"

   D. "Africa's People"

4. Which of the following did Ana probably **not** do to find information for her report?

   A. read websites from zoos

   B. read websites about giraffes

   C. read websites about African animals

   D. read websites by people who draw giraffes

5. What kind of information did Ana expect to find in the encyclopedia under the entry "giraffe"?

   A. information about animals that look like the giraffe

   B. information about giraffes and what they are like

   C. information about Africa

   D. information about the giraffe's ancestors

Write It Out Suppose you like to play basketball. You would like to find out more about the sport. List two reference sources you could use to learn about basketball. Tell what entries or words you would look up in each source.

6. _____

   _____

   _____

LESSON 2 — Organizational Features: Headings

> **WORDS TO KNOW**
> **Heading** a word or phrase used as a special title on top of a page or paragraph that tells you about the text

 **Review It!** Read the heading and the paragraph. How and why is the heading different from the rest of the paragraph?

Polar Bears

Polar bears live on ice and snow. Their thick fur keeps them warm even when they are wet from swimming after seals.

> **Hint** Notice that the heading **Polar Bears** appears in darker type than the rest of the paragraph. The heading tells you what the paragraph is about.

 **Try It!** Read this passage. As you read, <u>circle</u> the headings.

1. **Chapter 4: Bears**

   There are eight bear species in the world. Each kind of bear is special.

2. **Brown Bears**

   Brown bears range in color from cream to almost black. They are common in parts of North America. Brown bears love to eat fish.

3. **Giant Pandas**

   Giant pandas live in China. They live in bamboo forests and eat lots of bamboo.

4. **Sun Bears**

   Sun bears live in forests in Asia. These small bears have a yellow mark on their chest. Many people think the mark looks like a rising or setting sun.

   Now, use the passage to answer the questions on the following page.

1. What is the chapter about?

   A. polar bears   **C.** pandas

   B. bears   **D.** sun bears

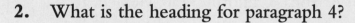

2. What is the heading for paragraph 4?

   A. Bears   **C.** Giant Pandas

   B. Brown Bears   **D.** Sun Bears

3. Which paragraph tells about brown bears?

   A. paragraph 1   **C.** paragraph 3

   B. paragraph 2   **D.** paragraph 4

4. Under which heading would you find information about what giant pandas eat?

   A. Bears

   B. Brown Bears

   C. Giant Pandas

   D. Sun Bears

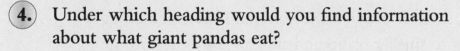

In Your Own Words

5. Read this sentence.

   Sun bears like to eat insects or tree sap.

   Which paragraph does this sentence belong in? Why?

   _____

   _____

   _____

1.
Where did you look to find out what the chapter was about?

4.
Where is all the information about pandas?

5.
What is the subject of this sentence?

On Your Own! Read this passage. Answer the questions that follow it.

Chapter 1: The Sonoran Desert

The Sonoran Desert covers parts of Arizona, California, and Mexico. It is filled with plants and animals that can survive in the hot, dry climate.

Cactuses

Many kinds of cactus grow in the Sonoran Desert. The barrel cactus has a barrel shape. It can be between five and eleven feet tall. The saguaro cactus has big, arm-like branches. Birds and animals eat the cactuses for food and water.

Trees

Ironwood and mesquite trees grow in the Sonoran Desert. These trees give shade and shelter to smaller plants and animals. Birds nest in the branches, and animals eat the trees' seeds.

Reptiles

What's a desert without a few snakes and lizards? Gila monsters and rattlesnakes both make homes in the Sonoran Desert. They like the hot sun that beats down and warms their bodies.

Mammals

Many mammals live in the desert, too. They have found ways to stay cool. Bigger animals like bighorn sheep and mountain lions live in high, cool places. Jackrabbits and foxes hunt for mice and other small animals.

1. What is the chapter about?
   A. desert plants
   B. the desert climate
   C. the Sonoran Desert
   D. desert mammals

2. What is the heading for paragraph 3?
   A. Mammals
   B. Trees
   C. Cactuses
   D. Reptiles

3. What is paragraph 2 about?

   A. cactuses of the desert

   B. mammals of the desert

   C. reptiles of the desert

   D. insects of the desert

4. In which paragraph can you find information about foxes that live in the Sonoran Desert?

   A. paragraph 2

   B. paragraph 3

   C. paragraph 4

   D. paragraph 5

5. Under what heading would this sentence **best** fit?

   Several reptiles lay their eggs in the warm desert sand.

   A. Cactuses

   B. Trees

   C. Reptiles

   D. Mammals

Write It Out Imagine the passage had a sixth paragraph with the heading **Insects**. List some details that might be included under **Insects**. Use the contents under the other headings in Chapter 1 to help you.

6. _____

   _____

   _____

   _____

   _____

   _____

   _____

   _____

LESSON 3 Graphic Features

WORDS TO KNOW **Graphics** tools that help readers better understand information. Charts and graphs are different kinds of graphics.

Review It! Read the chart and tell how many brothers Mia has.

Number of Brothers and Sisters

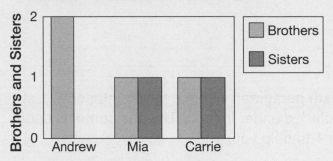

Hint Read the headings at the top of the chart. Find Mia's name and then read across.

Try It! Study this chart. As you read, <u>circle</u> the chart headings.

Animal	Where It Lives	What It Eats
bald eagle	North America	fish
lion	Africa	antelope, other small animals
dolphin	oceans of the world	fish, squid, shrimp
kangaroo	Australia	plants

Now, use the chart to answer the questions on the following page.

1. How many animals does the chart give information about?

   A. 1   **C.** 3

   B. 2   **D.** 4

2. According to the chart, what does a dolphin eat?

   A. plants

   B. fish

   C. fish, squid, shrimp

   D. antelope, other small animals

3. Where do lions live?

   A. North America

   B. Australia

   C. Africa

   D. South America

4. Which animal in the chart eats plants?

   A. antelope   **C.** bald eagle

   B. kangaroo   **D.** lion

In Your Own Words

5. What is another heading you could add to this chart?

_____

_____

_____

Ask Yourself

1.
How many rows do you see in the chart?

4.
Can you find the word *plants* in the chart and read across?

5.
What can you learn from reading the headings?

On Your Own!

Read this chart about a school. Answer the questions that follow it.

Teacher	Boys	Girls	Students' Favorite Animal	Students' Favorite Color
Mr. Young	13	12	cat	blue
Mrs. Garmon	11	13	dog	purple
Ms. Lee	10	15	dog	yellow
Mrs. Ortiz	12	11	hamster	blue
Mrs. Kelly	11	14	horse	red

1. How many girls are in Mrs. Garmon's class?

   A. 10
   B. 11
   C. 12
   D. 13

2. What color does Mr. Young's class like most?

   A. red
   B. blue
   C. yellow
   D. pink

3. Which class likes hamsters?

   A. Ms. Lee's class

   B. Mrs. Ortiz's class

   C. Mrs. Garmon's class

   D. Mrs. Kelly's class

4. Which class has the most boys?

   A. Mr. Young's class

   B. Mrs. Garmon's class

   C. Ms. Lee's class

   D. Mrs. Ortiz's class

5. Which class is the smallest?

   A. Mrs. Kelly's class

   B. Ms. Lee's class

   C. Mrs. Ortiz's class

   D. Mrs. Garmon's class

Write It Out List three pieces of information the chart gives you about each third-grade class.

6. _____

_____

_____

LESSON 4 Context Clues

WORDS TO KNOW | **Context clues** the words and sentences around or near an unknown word that help you figure out what the word means

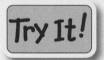 **Review It!** Read the sentences. Use context clues to figure out the word in dark type.

Jayne stopped at one cage and stared. The bird's head was covered in **scarlet** feathers. Jayne had never seen such a bright red color on an animal.

Hint The words "bright red color" in the last sentence help you figure out what *scarlet* means.

Try It! Read this passage. As you read, circle unfamiliar words. Underline any context clues that help you understand each word's meaning.

1 Many plants grow from seeds. Seeds hold all the parts of a new plant inside
2 them. But seeds cannot grow well if they are too close to the plant that
3 made them. The seeds and the plant **compete**, or fight, for the light,
4 water, and food they need. So seeds need to **journey** away from the plant.
5 How do they travel? Some seeds travel by wind. When wind blows, the
6 seeds **twirl** away like tiny spinning dancers. Other seeds travel by sticking
7 to passing people and animals. They **cling** to fur and clothes. Still other
8 seeds travel by water. They float along in ditches filled with rain.

Now, use the passage to answer the questions on the following page.

1. In line 3, what does the word *compete* mean?

    A. move   **C.** fight

    B. eat   **D.** grow

2. What does the word *journey* mean in line 4?

    A. walk

    B. travel

    C. dance

    D. need

> **1.**
> What words in the sentence help you understand the meaning of *compete?*

3. In line 6, the word *cling* means

    A. pass

    B. walk

    C. stick

    D. hide

> **2.**
> If you replace *journey* with each answer choice, which one makes sense in the sentence?

4. In line 5, the word *twirl* means

    A. spin

    B. hop

    C. run

    D. fall

In Your Own Words

5. What words helped you understand the meaning of *cling?*

_____

_____

_____

> **5.**
> What clues can you find in the sentence that comes before the one with *cling?*

On Your Own!

Read this passage. Answer the questions that follow it.

Mara sat on the floor and **glanced** around her bedroom. Everywhere she looked she saw mess. Toys were **scattered** here and there. Shelves were half full. Big cardboard boxes were half empty. She did like her new room. The sunny yellow walls were cheerful, and light **streamed** through two big windows. The problem was that the new room came with a new house—and a new school. Tomorrow would be her first day as the new kid, and Mara was filled with **dread**. That feeling of fear would go away, her mom said. Mara didn't believe it for a minute. She pulled a picture of her best friend out of a box and put it beside her.

A sudden knock on the door **startled** her, and she jumped. "Come in," she called.

A smiling face **emerged** from around the edge of the door. "Hi," the face said. "I'm Kyra. I live across the street."

Mara smiled back and felt her **gloomy** feelings begin to **vanish**. How could she stay sad with this friendly neighbor around?

---

1. What does the word *glanced* mean in this passage?

   A. looked
   B. walked
   C. cleaned
   D. played

2. What does the word *vanish* mean?

   A. disappear
   B. grow
   C. stay
   D. move

3. What does the word *scattered* mean?

    A. broken

    B. placed neatly

    C. lined up

    D. spread around

4. What does the word *gloomy* mean in this passage?

    A. sad

    B. silly

    C. happy

    D. angry

5. In this passage, what does the word *streamed* mean?

    A. ran

    B. flowed

    C. floated

    D. stopped

Write It Out Write the meaning for each word from the passage. Use the space provided in the chart.

6.

Word	Meaning
Dread	
Startled	
Emerged	

LESSON 5 Choosing the Right Texts

WORDS TO KNOW
Text a piece of published writing used for a purpose. When writing a report, you always want to pick the correct text.

Review It! Read these sentences. Use the Hint to help you figure out which text matches the student's purpose.

TJ needs to write a three-page report about spiders for science class. Should he look in a dictionary or an encyclopedia to find information?

Hint A dictionary will give TJ a definition of the word *spider*, but an encyclopedia will have a lot of information about different kinds of spiders.

Try It! Read these two passages from two different texts or books. As you read, underline the information that is the same in both.

Book 1

1. Spiders are not insects. They belong to a group of animals called arachnids.
2. A spider's body is divided into two parts. An insect's body is in three parts.
3. A spider has eight legs and eight eyes. An insect has six legs and two eyes.
4. Some spiders spin webs to catch insects.

Book 2

1. Garden spiders are web spiders. They use webs to catch their food. A garden
2. spider spins a web that looks like a wheel. It sits in the middle of the web.
3. When an insect lands on the web, the spider feels the movement.

Now, use the passage to answer the questions on the following page.

1. Both texts have information about

  A. garden spiders   C. insects' bodies

  B. spiders' bodies   D. spider webs

1.
What did you read about in both texts?

2. Book 1 would be helpful for a report about

  A. the differences between spiders and insects

  B. different kinds of spider webs

  C. different kinds of spiders

  D. spiders that hunt with webs

2.
What is Book 1 mainly about?

3. Book 2 would be helpful for a report about

  A. the differences between spiders and insects

  B. the group of animals called arachnids

  C. different kinds of spiders

  D. spiders that hunt without using webs

4. You want to learn more about garden spiders. The **best** source for information on garden spiders would be

  A. a dictionary entry for "garden spider"

  B. a newspaper article about spiders in your area

  C. an encyclopedia article about spiders

  D. a book about spiders that don't make webs

In Your Own Words

5. Suppose you are writing about how spiders hunt. List one detail from each book that would be most useful for your report.

5.
What did you learn about how spiders use their webs?

_____

_____

_____

On Your Own! Read these passages. Answer the questions that follow them.

Journal Entry 6

I have been on the Space Station for six days. My days follow a pattern. After sleep, I take a shower and eat breakfast. I usually eat warm scrambled eggs, but today I had cold cereal. It's quick and easy. I just add water to the cereal in the package, add milk and sugar, and it is ready to eat. Then I spend some time getting ready for the day's work. I clean and set up anything I will need to use for my jobs. I also try to get in my day's exercise before lunch. Lunch today was chicken and rice, my favorite!

from *Living on the Space Station*

What do the men and women living on the Space Station eat? Astronauts eat meals like macaroni and cheese, shrimp, and chicken with rice. They drink tea, coffee, and juice. Are the foods all in tubes? No. Many of the foods and drinks are dehydrated. That means all the water is taken out of them. To make their meals and drinks, the astronauts add water back to the foods. Each part of the meal can be stuck to a special tray. That keeps the food from floating away!

1. The book passage is mainly about

   A. food on space stations

   B. working in space

   C. making cereal

   D. how to dry out food

2. The journal entry and the book passage both tell about

   A. foods in tubes

   B. what people eat in space

   C. an astronaut's day in space

   D. different jobs in space

3. The journal entry would be most useful if you were writing about

   A. how astronauts live on the Space Station

   B. how to become an astronaut

   C. people's favorite foods in space

   D. how the Space Station works

4. The book passage would help you write about

   A. a day on the Space Station

   B. how long people stay on the Space Station

   C. what people eat on the Space Station

   D. where people cook on the Space Station

5. If you were writing about being an astronaut, what other text would be the **best** source for information?

   A. a book on the history of space travel

   B. a magazine article about training for astronauts

   C. an encyclopedia entry about space

   D. a newspaper article about the moon

Write It Out Tell how the journal entry is different from the book passage. List the reasons that they are different. Explain how the writers and their experiences make the passages different.

6. _____

_____

_____

_____

_____

_____

_____

LESSON 6 Asking Questions

WORDS TO KNOW **Questioning** a way of getting information as you read. Active readers ask themselves "What?" and "Why?" and other questions to better understand the text.

 Read the sentences. Use the Hint to ask yourself a "What?" or a "Why?" question as you read.

The little gray cat jumped up the steps. It looked through the screen door onto the porch. Things looked safe enough.

Hint You could ask yourself "What is the little cat doing?" or "Why is the little grey cat looking through the screen door?" to help you understand the cat's actions.

 Read the passage below. As you read, <u>write</u> a question that you have in the margin. <u>Circle</u> the answer when you find it.

(1) Many cities today have tall buildings called skyscrapers. But these tall buildings are a pretty new invention. Two things happened that led to the rise of the skyscraper.

(2) First, a man named Elisha Otis found a way to make elevators safe for people. Before Mr. Otis, elevators were used only to move goods in mines and factories.

(3) Next, Chicago grew rapidly in the late 1800s. The city began to run out of space for new buildings. The only way to find space was to build up. Using steel bars, builders invented a new way to support tall buildings. The skyscraper was born.

Now, use the passage to answer the questions on the following page.

1. What is the passage mainly about?

   A. Elisha Otis   **C.** skyscrapers

   B. Chicago   **D.** elevators

2. What question can you ask yourself about paragraph 1?

   A. What did Elisha Otis do?

   B. Why were skyscrapers first built?

   C. What holds up tall buildings?

   D. What did Chicago builders need to do?

2.
What does paragraph 1 give you information about?

3. What did Elisha Otis do?

   A. invented the elevator

   B. found a way to make elevators safer

   C. built the first skyscraper

   D. used huge steel bars in buildings

3.
In which paragraph do you read the information about Mr. Otis?

4. Which question would **not** be based on what you read in paragraph 3?

   A. Why did builders need to build up?

   B. What did builders use to support tall buildings?

   C. What happened in Chicago in the late 1800s?

   D. What were elevators first used for?

In Your Own Words

5. Write a "What?" or "Why?" question that came into your mind as you read the passage.

   _____

   _____

   _____

5.
What other information would you like to know about this topic?

On Your Own!

Read this passage. Answer the questions that follow it.

You have probably seen these little creatures hopping around in your yard or near a pond or at the zoo. But do you know which ones are frogs and which ones are toads? Frogs and toads have a lot in common, but they also have a few differences.

Frogs have long legs that are good for hopping. They also have smooth, wet skin and special pads on their toes that help them climb. Frogs are more likely to live near or in water. Toads have shorter legs and look thicker than frogs. They have drier skin that often has warty-looking bumps on it.

The hoppers are alike, though. Both have big round eyes that stick out from their heads. Their eyes help them see in most directions, which is important because they can't turn their heads like we can. Frogs and toads both eat insects, spiders, worms, and slugs.

Most frogs and toads lay their eggs in water. The eggs hatch into tadpoles, funny-looking things that look like little fish with really big heads. The tadpoles slowly grow legs and start to breathe air as they turn into little frogs and toads.

1. The passage is mainly about
   A. frogs
   B. tadpoles and frogs
   C. frogs and toads
   D. toads

2. Which paragraph would help answer questions about tadpoles?
   A. paragraph 1
   B. paragraph 2
   C. paragraph 3
   D. paragraph 4

3. Which paragraph would tell you why frogs have big round eyes?

　A. paragraph 1

　B. paragraph 2

　C. paragraph 3

　D. paragraph 4

4. Which question would be based on what you read in paragraph 2?

　A. What are tadpoles?

　B. What do toads look like?

　C. What do frogs and toads eat?

　D. What can frogs and toads not do?

5. Which question does paragraph 3 answer?

　A. How are frogs and toads alike?

　B. What do frogs and toads eat?

　C. Where do frogs lay their eggs?

　D. How do frogs and toads move?

Write It Out　Use the passage to help you write a brief answer to the question below.

6. What is the purpose of this passage?

_____

_____

_____

_____

_____

_____

_____

_____

_____

LESSON 7 Graphic Organizers

WORDS TO KNOW **Graphic organizers** help you arrange and see information in an organized way. Idea webs and sequence charts are two examples of graphic organizers.

Review It! Look at the idea web. Use the Hint to fill in the blank circle.

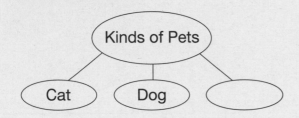

Kinds of Pets

Cat   Dog   ( )

Hint The topic is listed in the middle circle: Kinds of Pets. Two kinds of pets, cat and dog, are listed in the outside circles. What other kind of pet can you think of?

Try It! Read this passage. Circle the topic of the paragraph.

1 My family's visit to the Wonder Cave was exciting. The ranger led us
2 down a steep hill. Then we got on a kind of train that took us farther
3 down. Soon we were underground. The ranger gave us three rules to
4 remember: speak quietly, don't touch, and watch where you walk. The
5 first room of the cave was filled with huge rock forms. The ones called
6 stalagmites grew up from the floor. The ones called stalactites grew down
7 from the ceiling. In the next room, we saw tiny rock forms. The ranger said
8 they were called soda straws.

Now, use the passage to answer the questions on the following page.

1. What would you write in the middle circle of an idea web about the cave?

    A. rules   **C.** underground

    B. a park ranger   **D.** rock forms

2. Which one would you put into a smaller, outside circle?

    A. bats   **C.** stalagmites

    B. water   **D.** steep hill

    > **2.**
    > Once inside the cave, what did the family see?

3. Which one would you put into another outside circle?

    A. soda straws   **C.** train car

    B. drinking straws   **D.** tiny caves

4. What would be a good title for the passage, based on the idea web?

    A. Cave Rock Formations

    B. Cave Names

    C. Rooms in the Cave

    D. A Cave Visit

    > **4.**
    > What does a title tell a reader?

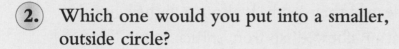

5. In your own words, explain what goes in the middle circle of a word web and what goes in the outside circles.

    _____

    _____

    _____

    > **5.**
    > Where do you put the topic? Where do you put **facts** related to the topic?

On Your Own!

Read this passage. Answer the questions that follow it.

Did you know that people have been chewing gum for hundreds of years? It's true! People who lived in Greece a long time ago chewed sap from a Greek plant. The sap cleaned their teeth. It also made their breath smell good! The Native Americans chewed sap from spruce trees. They taught the people in the colonies to chew it, too. Lumps of spruce sap were the first pieces of gum sold in the United States. People in Mexico chewed a rubbery gum from a native tree. It is called chicle.

A man in New York named Thomas Adams learned about chicle in the late 1800s. He knew people in Mexico chewed chicle. He tried a piece himself. He liked it! In 1870, Adams opened the world's first chewing gum factory. At first, gum did not have flavors added to it. But Adams made a gum called Black Jack. It was flavored like licorice. It was also the first gum sold as sticks instead of chunks. The only problem with Black Jack was that the flavor did not last. Another man named William White fixed the flavor problem. He added sugar and corn syrup to the chicle. Then he added peppermint flavor. The flavor lasted. Gum as we know it was born.

1. If you made an idea web about paragraph 1, what would go in the middle circle?

   A. People in Greece
   B. The First Chewing Gum
   C. Chicle
   D. Spruce Gum

2. What would **not** go in one of the outside circles?

   A. spruce sap
   B. peppermint
   C. mastic sap
   D. chicle

3. If you made a web for paragraph 2, what would you put in the middle circle?

   A. Black Jack
   B. Thomas Adams
   C. Native Americans
   D. people in Mexico

4. Which would you put in an outside circle?

   A. chicle
   B. New York
   C. flavors
   D. chunks

5. If you made a word web with William White in the middle circle, which of the following could go in an outside circle?

   A. chewed spruce gum
   B. invented gum
   C. added sugar and corn syrup
   D. sold gum in sticks

Write It Out Use what you know about idea webs to help you write a brief answer to the question below.

6. Your topic is ice cream flavors. Explain what you would put in **two** outside circles of an idea web and why.

_____

_____

_____

_____

_____

_____

_____

_____

LESSON 8 Main Idea

WORDS TO KNOW **Main idea** what a passage is mostly about

 Read the passage. Use the Hint to help you figure out the main idea of the passage.

Making banana bread is a simple process. You need two or three very ripe bananas and a few other ingredients. In just a few minutes, you'll be cooking!

Hint The sentences tell you about how to do something. What is it?

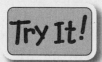 Read this passage. Underline sentences that tell you what the passage is about.

1. It's a leap year! Does that mean we leap all year? No, it means there is one extra day, February 29, added to the calendar. Leap years only happen every four years. Why do we have leap years? They make the calendar work.

2. There are 365 days in a year. Those 365 days mark the time it takes Earth to complete its orbit around the sun. But the actual time it takes Earth to make the trip is 365 and one quarter days. After four years, the calendar is off by one full day. To correct the problem, a leap day is added once every four years.

Now, use the passage to answer the questions on the following page.

1. What is the passage mostly about?

   A. the calendar   **C.** leap year
   B. Earth   **D.** time

2. Which sentence **best** states the main idea of the passage?

   A. There are 365 days in a year.
   B. Every four years, an extra day is added.
   C. Earth takes one year to travel around the sun.
   D. In a leap year, an extra day is added to the calendar.

3. What does the passage explain about leap years?

   A. why we have them
   B. why they are called leap years
   C. who came up with the idea
   D. how long they last

4. What is the **main** idea of paragraph 1?

   A. The extra day in a leap year is February 29.
   B. Leap years happen every four years.
   C. Leap years make the calendar work.
   D. We leap four times in leap years.

In Your Own Words

5. What does the passage teach you about our calendar?

   _____

   _____

   _____

Ask Yourself

2. What is the passage mostly about?

4. What is the most important idea in paragraph 1?

5. How long does it take Earth to travel around the sun?

On Your Own!

Read this passage. Answer the questions that follow it.

The next time you are hungry for a snack, don't grab the chips and soda. Find something that is good for you. These healthy snacks are easy and fun to make.

Do you like sweet snacks? Vanilla yogurt makes a great dip for fruit. Ask an adult to cut some apples for you, or just peel a banana and dip it in. If you like a little crunch, add some granola. If vanilla is not your flavor, use strawberry or peach yogurt. You can also add honey to plain yogurt for a "not too sweet" dip.

Looking for something salty to eat? Try putting a slice of turkey and some cream cheese on a wheat tortilla. Roll them up together. Then slice the roll into pieces. For something different, pop some plain popcorn in the microwave. Toss it with some grated cheese and chili powder. You made popcorn nachos!

Do you crave sweet and salty tastes at the same time? Mix up your own trail mix. Put raisins, peanuts, pretzels, and a few chocolate chips in a bowl. Make it fun. Snacking doesn't have to boring—and it doesn't have to be bad for you!

---

1. The passage is mostly about

    A. sweet snacks

    B. salty snacks

    C. healthful snacks

    D. eating snacks

2. What is the **main** idea of this passage?

    A. Everybody likes to make these snacks.

    B. Snacks can be easy, fun, and good for you.

    C. Some people only eat food that is good for them.

    D. Making snacks does not take very long.

3. What is paragraph 2 mostly about?

   A. sweet snacks that are easy to make

   B. salty snacks that are easy to make

   C. how to make fruit dip

   D. how to make popcorn

4. What is paragraph 4 mostly about?

   A. how to make good food choices

   B. how to make healthy snacks

   C. how to make your own trail mix

   D. how to keep growing

5. What would be a good title for this passage?

   A. I'm Hungry

   B. All Kinds of Food

   C. What Do You Like?

   D. Let's Make Healthy Snacks

Write It Out   Use the passage to help you write a brief answer to the question below.

6. How does the author most likely feel about snack foods?

   _____

   _____

   _____

LESSON 9 Supporting Details

WORDS TO KNOW   **Supporting details**   pieces of information in a passage that support, or tell about, the subject or main idea

---

Review It!   Read the sentences. Use the Hint to help you figure out which statement is a supporting detail.

Plants are living creatures. Like animals, they need water, air, and light.

Hint The main idea is that plants are living creatures. What details about this main idea do you learn in the next sentence?

Try It!   Read this passage. <u>Circle</u> the main idea. <u>Underline</u> supporting details that help you understand the main idea.

(1)   Exercise is an important part of a healthy life, even for kids. Kids who get plenty of exercise have stronger muscles and bones. They are better at dealing with the challenges that come up every day. They even sleep better.

(2)   When adults think of exercise, they think of going to a gym or running around a track. But kids get exercise when they play. Think about recess. You run and jump. You go across the monkey bars. You bend over to pick up balls or tie your shoes. Those things are all exercise. They help kids just like you grow strong. So get out there and play!

Now, use the passage to answer the questions on the following page.

1. According to the beginning of the passage, exercise is

 A. fun   **C.** hard work

 B. healthy   **D.** dull

2. Which of the following is a detail from the passage that supports the main idea?

 A. Kids who exercise deal better with daily challenges.

 B. Grownups exercise at the gym or on the track.

 C. Most kids like to exercise by being on teams.

 D. Everyone should exercise more than they do.

3. Which of the following is **not** a supporting detail from the passage?

 A. Kids who exercise sleep better.

 B. Kids do not get enough exercise.

 C. Kids get exercise by playing.

 D. Kids who exercise have strong bones.

4. What do the details in the passage have in common?

 A. They're all about kids.

 B. They're all about the benefit of exercise.

 C. They're all about sports.

 D. They're all about ways to have fun.

In Your Own Words

5. What do the supporting details teach you about exercise?

_____

_____

_____

2. Which of the answer choices helps you understand the **main** idea of the passage?

4. What are the most important words in the details?

5. What is the main idea of the passage? Which sentence helped you understand the main idea?

On Your Own!

Read this passage. Answer the questions that follow it.

Bees are insects that most people have seen. You know they buzz. You know some of them make honey. But there is a lot of information about bees that people don't know.

Bees are insects that may be several sizes and colors. The biggest bee is 1.6 inches long. The smallest bee is only .07 inches long. That's about two millimeters! All bees are covered in hair. Bees can be black or brown, and some bees have yellow or orange stripes. The most colorful bee is the orchid bee. It is bright green, blue, and red.

Without bees, many of the plants we enjoy would not be around. Bees eat pollen and nectar from plants. Pollen is the yellow dust you see in the middle of flowers. Nectar is the sweet liquid that some plants make. Bees that make honey use the nectar to do their job. The bees fly from flower to flower. As they go, pollen gets spread from one plant to another. This is what lets the plants reproduce, or make new plants.

1. The **main** idea of this passage is that

   A. bees are fascinating
   B. bees make honey
   C. bees are black or brown
   D. bees eat pollen

2. Paragraph 2 is mainly about

   A. what colors bees are
   B. what bees look like
   C. how big a bee can get
   D. orchid bees

3. One detail that helps you understand the **main** idea of paragraph 2 is

   A. bees come in several sizes and colors

   B. bees are very interesting insects

   C. the biggest bee is 1.6 inches long

   D. some people are afraid of bees

4. Which of the following is the **main** idea of paragraph 3?

   A. Plants make other plants.

   B. Pollen grows in plants.

   C. Bees make honey.

   D. Plants need bees.

5. Which detail supports the **main** idea of paragraph 3?

   A. Plants need bees.

   B. Bees spread pollen from plant to plant.

   C. Bees are fascinating.

   D. Honey bees make beeswax.

Write It Out Use the passage to help you write a brief answer to the question below.

6. What are **two** more details from paragraph 3 that help you understand the **main** idea?

   _____

   _____

   _____

LESSON

10 Making Inferences

WORDS TO
KNOW
Inference an educated guess about a passage based on information you read plus information you already know

---

Read the sentences. Use the Hint to help you make an inference about the setting.

Jana pushed her chair in slowly and stood up. She grabbed her backpack just as the bell rang.

Hint What can you infer about where Jana is? Use what you know and what you read to make the inference.

Try It! Read this passage. <u>Underline</u> sentences that help you understand something not directly stated in the passage.

(1) Max climbed up the bus steps slowly and dropped into the first seat he
(2) saw. He kept his head down. He didn't want to talk to anybody, not even
(3) James. He knew James would ask what was wrong. Max wasn't sure he
(4) could explain it to somebody like James. James had lived in one place his
(5) whole life. Max had never lived anywhere for longer than a year. He had
(6) been to four schools in four years. He had thought this school would be
(7) okay. But after what happened in the lunchroom, he wasn't so sure.

Now, use the passage to answer the questions on the following page.

Ask Yourself

1. What can you infer about Max and James?

   A. They don't know each other.

   B. They don't like each other.

   C. They are friends.

   D. They are brothers.

1.
What does Max think about James? How can you tell?

2. How does Max feel about changing schools every year?

   A. He thinks it is fun.

   B. He thinks it is exciting.

   C. He thinks it is awful.

   D. He thinks it is boring.

2.
How would you feel if you changed schools every year? How would it feel to be the new kid all the time?

3. What can you infer about Max's day at school?

   A. It was a bad day.   C. It was his first day.

   B. It was a fun day.   D. It was his last day.

4. What happened in the lunchroom made Max

   A. shy   C. tired

   B. happy   D. unhappy

In Your Own Words

5. What words and phrases in the passage help you understand how Max is feeling when he gets on the bus?

   _____

   _____

   _____

5.
What clues does the author give you? How does Max act? What are his thoughts?

On Your Own!

Read this passage. Answer the questions that follow it.

Clara took off her apron and hung it on the peg. She had finished peeling the potatoes that Mama had left for her. Now it was time to get the eggs from the nests in the barn. She needed to have her chores done before Mama and Papa got back from town. They had taken the wagon early this morning and would not be home until dark. Five miles was a long way to go, but they needed supplies from Mr. Smitt's store.

Clara could hear the sound of an ax hitting wood. Her brother had his chores to do. As she walked to the barn, she listened for the other normal sounds of life. But there were no sounds. The animals were all quiet. The trees that were usually swishing and swaying in the wind were still. Clara looked up at the sky and frowned. Big, black clouds had blocked the sun. These didn't look like regular rain clouds, though.

"Ethan?" she called. "I think it's going to—ow!" Clara grabbed the egg basket and ran for the barn. Hail! Clara thought. Oh, no! Where were Mama and Papa right now?

---

1. You can infer that Clara lives

    A. on a farm

    B. in a barn

    C. in a small house

    D. near her friends

2. Clara **most likely** feels that her chores are

    A. too hard for her to finish

    B. a waste of time

    C. silly and boring

    D. a normal part of life

3. Why does Clara say "ow!"?

   A. A chicken pecked her.

   B. Hail hit her on the head.

   C. She dropped the egg basket.

   D. A piece of wood hit her.

4. At the end of the passage, Clara is

   A. excited

   B. angry

   C. worried

   D. happy

5. You can infer that the story takes place

   A. in modern times

   B. a long time ago

   C. in a big city

   D. at a school

Write It Out   Use the story to help you write a brief answer to the question below.

6. What kind of person is Clara? Give **two** details from the passage that helped you make the inference.

   _____

   _____

   _____

LESSON 11 Drawing Conclusions

WORDS TO KNOW — **Conclusion** your own idea or opinion about what you read in a passage. Like an inference, a conclusion is based on clues in the reading and what you already know.

 **Review It!** Read the sentences. Use the Hint to help you draw a conclusion about what has happened.

Tim frowned at the shoes all over his room. They all had rips and holes in them. His brother had promised to keep the puppy out. Now his room was a wreck—again!

Hint What do you think has happened? Can you conclude that it has happened other times?

Try It! Read this passage. Underline clues in the sentences that help you draw conclusions about something in the passage.

1   "Now that is a good project," said Min Ju. She looked over her notes one last time. She was pretty sure everything was done, but it was always a good idea to check. This was the hardest science project she had done. She wanted to win another blue ribbon in the science fair. So she checked everything again. Pictures? Yes. Daily journal? Yes. Problem clearly written? Yes. Results? Yes.

2   "Min Ju?" her mom called up the stairs. "We need to leave for school in about five minutes. You need time to set everything up. Is Fluffy in her cage and ready to go?"

Now, use the passage to answer the questions on the following page.

1. How does Min Ju probably feel about the science fair?

   A. excited and sure she will do well

   B. nervous and unwilling to go

   C. upset that she has to be part of it

   D. unhappy and sure she will not win

2. Min Ju's project is probably

   A. not carefully done

   B. neat and well-planned

   C. sloppy and not finished

   D. the same as everyone else's

3. You can conclude that Min Ju is **most likely**

   A. bored in school   C. a good student

   B. nine years old   D. part of a large family

4. Who or what is Fluffy?

   A. Min Ju's stuffed dog   C. a hamster

   B. a small pet   D. Min Ju's favorite toy

 In Your Own Words

5. What clues in the passage helped you answer question 3?

   _____

   _____

   _____

1.
Does Min Ju expect to do well? How do you feel when you think you will be successful at something?

4.
What clues about Fluffy does the passage provide? What animals do people put in cages when going out?

5.
What does the passage tell you about Min Ju?

On Your Own!   Read this passage. Answer the questions that follow it.

Tony scooted back up against the wall and tried to disappear. He didn't want Dr. Kim to even see him. But it was too late. "Here you go," Dr. Kim said. "It's your turn." He didn't reach out like his classmates had. He shook his head a little. "Go ahead," Dr. Kim said. She held the big, furry spider on her hand out to Tony. "He won't hurt you, I promise."

"No, no thanks," he said. "I don't really like spiders all that much." He heard Jack snort next to him. He could almost guess what Jack was going to say next.

"Hey, what's the matter? Are you scared of the little spider, Tony?" Jack laughed. "No, I'm not scared," Tony said. "I just don't like spiders all that much." No way was he going to admit that spiders scared him to death. And no way was he going to let Jack make fun of him in front of everybody.

"No problem. I feel the same way about snakes," Dr. Kim said and moved on. Sherrie patted his back and said quietly, "I vote we go to the museum for our next trip. Nothing there can move!"

1. Where does the story take place?

   A. in a classroom at school

   B. on a field trip to the zoo

   C. on the playground at school

   D. at Tony's house

2. You can conclude that Jack is probably

   A. Tony's best friend

   B. kind to everyone

   C. a bully

   D. scared of spiders

3. What can you conclude about Tony?

   A. He can stand up for himself.

   B. He is afraid of Jack.

   C. He does not have many friends.

   D. He is scared of Dr. Kim.

4. What conclusion can you draw about Dr. Kim?

   A. She does not like children.

   B. She is worried about Tony.

   C. She is a kind person.

   D. She does not like spiders.

5. You can conclude that Sherrie

   A. doesn't like animals much

   B. only likes museums

   C. is scared of spiders

   D. does not like Tony

Write It Out   Use the passage to help you write a brief answer to the question below.

6. What conclusion can you draw about how Tony feels at the end of the passage?

_____

_____

_____

LESSON 12 Fact and Opinion

WORDS TO KNOW **Fact** a statement that is true and can be proved. **Opinion** a statement that gives someone's feelings about something. An opinion cannot be proved.

Review It!

Read the sentences. Use the Hint to help you find the opinion.

This year's parade went down 4th Street and ended at City Park. It was the best parade the city has ever seen.

Hint "The parade went down 4th Street" is a statement that can be proven. Can the writer's feelings about the parade be proven?

Try It!

Read this passage. <u>Underline</u> statements that are opinions.

(1) "Class," said Mr. Kelly, "let's talk about this year's play. The play will be about George Washington. I think it will be fun to do a play about him. He's very interesting. Who can tell me something about George Washington?"

(2) Grace said, "He was our first president. He was our best president."

(3) Danny said, "He was in the army. He led soldiers against England. He wore a white wig."

(4) "Wow, you guys know a lot," said Mr. Kelly. "Now let's learn some more."

Now, use the passage to answer the questions on the following page.

1. Which statement from the passage is an **opinion**?

   A. He was our first president.

   B. He wore a white wig.

   C. He's very interesting.

   D. He was in the army.

2. Which statement from the passage is a **fact**?

   A. He's very interesting.

   B. He was our best president.

   C. I think it will be fun to do a play about him.

   D. The play will be about George Washington.

3. What is Mr. Kelly's **opinion** about George Washington?

   A. He was the first president.

   B. He is interesting.

   C. He was the best president.

   D. He was in the army.

In Your Own Words

4. John wants the class play to be about someone else. He thinks George Washington is not interesting. Is this a **fact** or an **opinion**? How do you know?

   _____

   _____

   _____

1.
Which one tells what somebody thinks or feels?

2.
Which one can be proved true?

4.
Can John prove that George Washington is **not** interesting?

On Your Own!

Read this passage. Answer the questions that follow it.

Hey, kids! Are you ready for the best day of your life? Then tell your parents it's time for a trip to Wild Water World! This water park is the stuff of dreams. We have 50 different slides and rides. There is something here for everyone. Do you like speed? Then the Rolling Rapids are for you. *Water Park Weekly* called this ride "a blast!" Do you like something more peaceful? How about the Lazy River? Hop in a tube and float down a mile of river. You'll float past ducks and turtles. You'll see beautiful trees and flowers. You can even pick up one of our fabulous lunches to take along with you. Try our delicious sandwiches and perfectly made shakes. And what about you surfers out there? We have the newest wave machine available today. You'll feel like you're riding the big ones out in the ocean. Yes, we have it all. We have tubes, slides, waves, boards, and mats. We have pools and playgrounds. We have snacks and drinks. Nothing could be more fun than a day at Wild Water World. You'll want to spend your whole summer with us!

1. Which statement is a **fact** from the passage?

   A. This water park is the stuff of dreams.

   B. We have 50 different slides and rides.

   C. You'll see beautiful trees and flowers.

   D. There is something here for everyone.

2. Which statement is an **opinion** from the passage?

   A. We have the newest wave machine available today.

   B. We have tubes, slides, waves, boards, and mats.

   C. You'll float past ducks and turtles.

   D. Try our delicious sandwiches and perfectly made shakes.

3. Read this statement from the passage.

   We have pools and playgrounds.

   You can tell this statement is a **fact** because

   A. all water parks have pools and playgrounds

   B. I have seen a water park with pools and playgrounds

   C. it can be proved true

   D. it sounds like it might be true

4. Which of the following is an **opinion**?

   A. You'll have the best day ever at Wild Water World.

   B. Thousands of people visit the park every week.

   C. The park has food and drinks.

   D. Wild Water World is open every day from 9 A.M. until 6 P.M.

5. Read this statement from the passage.

   You'll want to spend your whole summer with us!

   You can tell this statement is an **opinion** because

   A. it can't be proven

   B. it is a true statement

   C. everyone likes water parks

   D. no one likes water parks

Write It Out   *Water World Weekly* said, "The Rolling Rapids ride is 'a blast.'" Is that a fact or an opinion? How can you tell?

6. _____

   _____

   _____

   _____

   _____

LESSON 13 Compare and Contrast

WORDS TO KNOW **Compare** to tell how things are alike **Contrast** to tell how things are different

Read the sentences. Use the Hint to help you compare and contrast the two brothers.

Jake is nine years old. His brother Jim is twelve. Jake's favorite sport is soccer. Jim's is basketball. The boys love to fly kites in the park.

Hint Think about the two boys' favorite sports. Are they the same? What do both boys love to do?

Try It! Read this passage. Underline statements that are opinions.

1. Can you tell the difference between a moth and a butterfly? They both
2. have wings. They both have antennae, or long, skinny feelers, on their
3. heads. They both drink nectar from flowers. But there are ways to tell
4. the two apart. Moths have thick antennae that look like feathers. Most
5. butterflies have long, smooth antennae. Moths also have bigger, fuzzier
6. bodies. Moths fly mostly at night. Butterflies fly mostly during the day.
7. Both insects rest by landing on leaves or flowers. But they rest in different
8. ways. Butterflies hold their wings up and against each other when they rest.
9. Moths flatten their wings out.

Now, use the passage to answer the questions on the following page.

1. What **two** things are being compared and contrasted?

   A. antennae and bodies   **C.** moths and butterflies

   B. wings and nectar   **D.** butterflies and insects

2. What is the same about moths and butterflies?

   A. Both have smooth antennae.

   B. Both rest with their wings flat.

   C. Both have very fuzzy bodies.

   D. Both drink nectar from flowers.

3. How are moths different from butterflies?

   A. They have bigger bodies.

   B. They fly during the day.

   C. They rest on leaves and flowers.

   D. They are insects.

4. How are butterflies different from moths?

   A. They fly during the night.

   B. They drink nectar.

   C. They have smooth antennae.

   D. They are insects.

In Your Own Words

5. Think of **two** animals that are both alike and different. Write **one** way they are alike and **one** way they are different.

_____

_____

_____

Ask Yourself

1. The paragraph tells how **two** things are alike and different. What are the **two** things?

2. Which answer is true about both moths and butterflies?

5. What interests you about each animal?

On Your Own!

Read this passage. Answer the questions that follow it.

Emma looked at her twin sister Kayla. She frowned. Kayla was wearing brown pants and a blue shirt. Emma had picked the same clothes from her side of the closet. That was the problem with being twins. She liked a lot of the same things as her sister. But she was tired of people saying they were so alike all the time. They were very different in some ways! Yes, they both liked dogs and the color blue. Yes, they both liked to ride horses and to swim. But Emma did not like cats and Kayla did. Kayla did not like to go camping and Emma did. They didn't really even look totally alike. If people would look closely, they'd see that Emma's eyes were brown and Kayla's were blue.

"Kayla," Emma said, "that's what I wanted to wear."

"So wear it," Kayla said. "It's okay if we wear the same thing."

"No, it's not," Emma replied. "I'm tired of people thinking we're totally alike!"

"Emma, it's not a big deal. We are a lot alike. Did you forget we're twins?"

---

1. Which **two** things are being compared and contrasted?

    A. blue eyes and brown eyes

    B. cats and dogs

    C. Emma and Kayla

    D. brothers and sisters

2. What do Emma and Kayla both like?

    A. swimming

    B. pink

    C. cats

    D. camping

3. What does Emma like but **not** Kayla?

    A. blue

    B. horses

    C. camping

    D. cats

4. What does Kayla like but **not** Emma?

    A. dogs

    B. cats

    C. horses

    D. swimming

5. In what way do Kayla and Emma look different?

    A. They are different heights.

    B. They like different clothes.

    C. Their hair is different colors.

    D. Their eyes are different colors.

Write It Out   Use the passage to help you write a brief answer to the question below.

6. People think the twins are just alike. How does Emma feel about that? How does Kayla feel?

_____

_____

_____

LESSON 14 Sequence

Sequence   the order in which events happen

 **Review It!**   Read the sentences. Use the Hint to help you number them in the correct sequence.

Put the pieces of bread together. Put peanut butter and jelly on one slice. Get out two slices of bread.

Hint To make a peanut butter and jelly sandwich, you follow a certain sequence. What do you need to do first? Next? Last?

 **Try It!**   Read this passage. <u>Circle</u> words or phrases that tell you the order in which things happen.

(1) Good grief, thought Meg. What an awful day! First, her alarm had not gone
(2) off. She was late and missed the bus. Then she had to wait for her brother
(3) to get ready. He was slow, and she was late for school. School itself was not
(4) any better. The test in science was really hard. At least after science was art.
(5) That was the best part of the day. She liked the project she was working
(6) on. But after art was a spelling test, and Meg was NOT a good speller.
(7) Finally it was time to go home. She was so glad to see her mom waiting for
(8) her after school!

Now, use the passage to answer the questions on the following page.

1. What happened after Meg's alarm didn't go off?

   A. She missed the bus.

   B. She took a science test.

   C. She went to art class.

   D. She saw her mom waiting.

2. When did Meg go to art?

   A. before school   C. on her way home

   B. after science   D. on Mondays

3. What happened after art?

   A. She took a science test.

   B. She missed the bus.

   C. She took a spelling test.

   D. She went home.

4. When did Meg see her mom?

   A. when she got home

   B. when school ended

   C. right after science

   D. right after she missed the bus

Ask Yourself

1. What does the fourth sentence say?

2. Find *art* in the story. When did art happen?

5. What clue word helps you figure out the sequence?

In Your Own Words

5. Use information from the passage to complete the sequence chart.

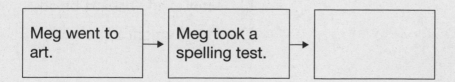

Meg went to art. → Meg took a spelling test. → [ ]

Read this passage. Answer the questions that follow it.

On Friday afternoon Danny asked his grandmother what she would like for her birthday. She asked him to make something for her. Make something? Danny thought. What can I make? That night he asked Dad to help him think of something to make.

"Well," Dad said. "I know she likes to have a sweet treat now and then. Why don't you make her a birthday cake?"

Mom was listening. "Cakes are pretty hard if you've never made one. How about banana bread? It's a tasty treat, and it's easy to make. I'll help you if you need me."

The next day Mom and Danny looked up a recipe for banana bread. Then they went to the store and bought all the ingredients. When they got home, Danny followed the steps in the recipe. He started by mixing the dry ingredients together. Next, he mashed the bananas. He added them, two eggs, and oil to the dry mix. Then he stirred it all together. Mom didn't need to help until it was time to pour the batter into the pan. Then she put the pan in the oven. Soon the whole kitchen smelled great.

That night Danny gave Gran her present. She loved every bite!

1. What happened first in the story?
   A. Danny talked to Dad.
   B. Danny went shopping.
   C. Danny made banana bread.
   D. Danny talked to Gran.

2. What happened right before Danny and Mom went to the store?
   A. They found a recipe.
   B. They talked with Dad.
   C. They made banana bread.
   D. They bought ingredients

3. Danny talked with Gran. When did he talk to Dad?

    A. that same afternoon

    B. that night

    C. the next day

    D. the next night

4. What did Danny do first to follow the recipe?

    A. mixed the dry ingredients

    B. mashed the bananas

    C. added eggs and oil

    D. poured the batter

5. When did Mom help?

    A. after the bread was done

    B. before the bread was mixed

    C. before Danny stirred all the ingredients

    D. after Danny stirred all the ingredients

Write It Out Use information from the passage to fill in the sequence chart.

6.

Gran asked Danny to make something.	→		→		→	Danny gave Gran her present.

LESSON 15 Author's Perspective

WORDS TO KNOW **Author's perspective** what an author feels and believes about the topic. Sometimes an author's perspective shows **bias**, an opinion that keeps the writer from seeing any other viewpoint.

Review It!

Read the passage. Use the Hint to figure out the author's perspective.

It's about time the city tore down that old building on Main Street. I feel that the idea it can be turned into anything useful is just silly.

> **Hint** Think about how the writer feels about the old building. Does he or she think it's worth saving?

Try It!

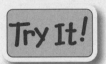

Read this passage. <u>Underline</u> statements that help you understand the author's perspective. <u>Circle</u> any words that show bias.

(1) As a business owner, I believe it is time to charge more for parking
(2) downtown. We charge $5.00 for the entire day. Other cities near us charge
(3) up to $10.00 per day. It is important to our downtown businesses to have
(4) parking available for our customers. Right now, people are paying to park
(5) and leaving their cars in one spot all day. That leaves little parking space for
(6) customers, and I feel this is driving business away from my door. It is time
(7) for our city leaders to speak up for business owners.

Now, use the passage to answer the questions on the following page.

1. What does the author believe about parking downtown?

   A. Parking costs too much.

   B. Parking costs too little.

   C. There are too few parking spaces.

   D. There are too many parking spaces.

2. What word in the passage helps you know you are reading about the writer's feelings?

   A. believe   **C.** charge

   B. time   **D.** business

3. Which statement **best** expresses the author's perspective?

   A. People should shop downtown.

   B. The city leaders are doing a bad job.

   C. Lack of parking space hurts businesses downtown.

   D. Other cities charge more for parking.

4. The writer of this passage

   A. thinks all drivers who come downtown are the same

   B. is concerned about the success of the business

   C. is trying to get business from readers

   D. is trying to persuade readers to come downtown

In Your Own Words

5. Suppose the writer was a person who worked in a store downtown. How would the writing be different?

Ask Yourself

1.
What point is the writer trying to make in the passage?

2.
Can you find a word in the passage that indicates you are reading about someone's **opinion** about a topic?

5.
If you were a worker, would you want to pay a lot or a little to park your car?

On Your Own!

Read this passage. Answer the questions that follow it.

I went for a walk around Town Lake Park yesterday. It was a beautiful afternoon and a perfect day to be outside. Sadly, my walk was ruined by the thoughtless behavior of others. I firmly believe it is time for dogs to be banned from the lake and the park around it. Dog owners have shown again and again that they care more for their pets than for people. They all refuse to clean up after their animals.

The city has placed signs all along the lake trails asking dog owners to do the right thing. It seems as though none of them can read, or they choose to ignore the signs. This is not just a problem for me. When animal waste is left on the ground, it washes into the lake with every storm. It also soaks into the ground and down into our groundwater. The lake is our main source of drinking water. Many people drill wells to tap into the groundwater. Animal waste pollutes both sources of water.

I understand that people love their pets and enjoy walking with them. I myself do not care for dogs. But there are other parks in town that are better suited for dogs. Town Lake Park is a lovely part of our area. Let's not ruin it.

---

1. What is the author's perspective in this passage?

   A. People should not walk their dogs.

   B. Dogs should not be allowed in any park.

   C. Dogs make poor pets.

   D. People should do a better job cleaning up after their dogs.

2. Each of the following word clues shows how the writer feels about the topic **except**

   A. sadly

   B. thoughtless

   C. waste

   D. ruin

3. Which of these is a **fact** the writer uses to support his perspective?

   A. The lake is our main source of drinking water.

   B. They all refuse to clean up after their animals.

   C. It seems as though none of them can read.

   D. Town Lake Park is a lovely part of our area.

4. What statement by the writer shows bias?

   A. I went for a walk around Town Lake Park yesterday.

   B. It was a beautiful afternoon.

   C. This is not just a problem for me.

   D. I personally do not care for dogs

5. When the writer says that "Dog owners…care more for their pets than for people," this suggests that

   A. all dog owners are alike

   B. it has been proven that dog owners care more for their pets than for people

   C. we should care more for each other than for pets

   D. the writer is a pet lover

Write It Out   Use the passage to help you write a brief answer to the question below.

6. What **fact** or detail could the writer add to support his perspective?

   _____

   _____

   _____

   _____

   _____

   _____

Telling the Genres Apart

WORDS TO KNOW

Genre a category, or type, of writing. Novels and stories are fiction. Plays or dramas are almost all dialogue. Nonfiction is based on facts. Poetry has lines and may rhyme.

 Review It! Read the paragraph and figure out the genre that is being described.

Jan enjoys reading books about real people and their careers. She hopes that reading these books will help her decide what she wants to do when she grows up.

> **Hint** Here, the phrase *books about real people* helps you understand that Jan likes to read nonfiction.

Try It! Read this passage. As you read, <u>underline</u> words and phrases that help you figure out each genre that is being described.

1. Our class was going to the library this afternoon. Before we went,
2. Mrs. Gomez, our teacher, had a discussion with us. She wanted to know
3. what kinds of books we found interesting. Jill explained that she liked
4. books about funny animals that acted just like people. Jake was searching
5. for a book about how to care for puppies, because he had a brand-new
6. puppy at home. Rose was the class poet, and she wrote wonderful rhymes.
7. So it was easy to guess what kind of book she was after! At the library, we
8. all found the books we wanted.

Now, use the passage to answer the questions on the following page.

1. This passage is an example of

   A. a poem   **C.** science

   B. fiction   **D.** drama

1.

What features in the passage help you identify the genre?

2. On lines 4–6, the book Jake is looking for is

   A. drama   **C.** poetry

   B. fiction   **D.** nonfiction

2.

Does Jill enjoy reading about real animals or animals that are made up?

3. The sentence on lines 3–4 shows that Jill likes

   A. nonfiction

   B. drama

   C. fiction

   D. poetry

4. How can you tell Rose wants poetry?

   A. She writes poems herself.

   B. She says so in the passage.

   C. She doesn't like anything else.

   D. There are no other books available.

In Your Own Words

5. Compare and contrast the kind of book Jill wants with the kind of book Jake wants.

   _____

   _____

   _____

5.

How are the **two** kinds of books alike? How are they different?

Reading Literature

Read this passage. Answer the questions that follow it.

Rita belonged to a book club with five friends. Every two weeks, the group would meet to discuss a book they had read. It was fun to talk about different kinds of books and to share their thoughts. The book they were discussing this week was *How Animals Survive*. Everyone liked this book because they learned a lot of information about how animals in the wild stay safe.

The book club had been meeting for several months. So by now, the members had read more than a dozen books. Here are some of the other titles they had read: *The Life of Martin Luther King, Jr.; Billy's Special Birthday; Lion Goes to Market; Ways to Travel;* and *Rhymes for Fun Times*.

"We need to figure out what to read next," Rita said to the group. "So far, we have read fiction, nonfiction, and poems. I have an idea for our next book. The title is *Let's Put on a Play!* We can read the book and then perform one of the plays!" The rest of the group thought it was an excellent idea.

1. Which book from the passage is a book of poems?

    A. *Lion Goes to Market*

    B. *Billy's Special Birthday*

    C. *Rhymes for Fun Times*

    D. *Ways to Travel*

2. Which of the following pairs of books are nonfiction?

    A. *The Life of Martin Luther King, Jr.* and *Ways to Travel*

    B. *How Animals Survive* and *Billy's Special Birthday*

    C. *Ways to Travel* and *Rhymes for Fun Times*

    D. *How Animals Survive* and *Lion Goes to Market*

3. Which of the following pairs of books are fiction?

    A. *Billy's Special Birthday* and *How Animals Survive*

    B. *Rhymes for Fun Times* and *Let's Put on a Play!*

    C. *Lion Goes to Market* and *Ways to Travel*

    D. *Lion Goes to Market* and *Billy's Special Birthday*

4. Which book from the passage contains drama?

    A. *How Animals Survive*

    B. *Let's Put on a Play!*

    C. *The Life of Martin Luther King, Jr.*

    D. *Lion Goes to Market*

5. Read the following book titles from the passage:

    The Life of Martin Luther King, Jr.

    Billy's Special Birthday

    Lion Goes to Market

    Which of the following statements is true about these books?

    A. There are more nonfiction books than fiction books.

    B. There are more drama books than fiction books.

    C. There are more fiction books than nonfiction books.

    D. There are no nonfiction books.

Write It Out   Use the passage to help you write an answer to the question below.

6. According to the passage, which kind of book does the group read most? Write the titles on the lines below. Then write the title of a book you have read recently.

    _____

    _____

    _____

Reading Literature

LESSON 17 Author's Purpose

WORDS TO KNOW

Author's purpose the reason an author writes something. An author may write to entertain, give information, explain how to do something, or to express an opinion.

Review It! Read the paragraph and figure out the author's purpose for writing it.

This healthful snack is easy to make. First, mix yogurt and blueberries. Next, mix in almonds. Last, sprinkle granola on top.

> **Hint** Here, the phrase *easy to make* and the words *first, next,* and *last* help you understand the author's purpose.

Try It! Read this passage. As you read, <u>underline</u> words and phrases that help you understand the author's purpose.

1 Emperor penguins are the largest penguins. These seabirds can't fly, but
2 they are excellent swimmers. Most emperor penguins live in Antarctica
3 where the weather is frigid. However, a thick layer of fat and feathers keeps
4 them warm. Another way these birds stay warm is by huddling in groups.
5 These smart penguins take turns moving to the center of the group where
6 it is warmest. Emperor penguins can also be very playful. They enjoy
7 running, hopping, jumping, and sliding down hills on their bellies.

Now, use the passage to answer the questions on the following page.

Reading Literature

1. Why did the author write this passage?

    A. to give an opinion   **C.** to make you laugh

    B. to give information   **D.** to give directions

1.
Which key words helped you figure out the author's purpose?

2. Which of the following facts did you learn from the passage?

    A. Emperor penguins eat small fish.

    B. Emperor penguins have short necks.

    C. Emperor penguins have round eyes.

    D. Emperor penguins are excellent swimmers.

2.
How did you identify the **facts** in this passage?

3. In this passage, the author's main goal is to

    A. share facts about Antarctica

    B. make fun of emperor penguins

    C. share facts about emperor penguins

    D. explain why emperor penguins are playful

4. Which word is **not** used to describe emperor penguins?

    A. brave   **C.** smart

    B. excellent   **D.** playful

In Your Own Words

5. How does the author feel about emperor penguins?

_____

_____

_____

5.
Why would you choose to write about a particular animal?

Reading Literature

Read this passage. Answer the questions that follow it.

Have you ever stayed up later than you should at night? If you have, then you know that not getting enough sleep can make you feel tired and grumpy the next day. You may also notice that you can't think clearly and have trouble paying attention.

Scientists have found that getting a good night's sleep helps people do their best during the day, both at school and at work. Everyone needs sleep to stay healthy and feel alert. Children need more sleep than adults because they are still growing. They require at least nine hours of sleep a night. However, studies show that many children do not get enough sleep. When you don't get the sleep you need, it can affect your ability to learn.

What can you do to help you get a good night's sleep? First, go to bed at the same time each night. Second, do a quiet activity before going to sleep. It will help make you drowsy. Remember, getting enough sleep is one of the best things you can do for your body. So from now on, make sure you go to bed on time!

---

1. **Why did the author write this passage?**

   A. to entertain

   B. to tell about her life

   C. to make you sad

   D. to share an opinion

2. **What does the author think you should do before bedtime?**

   A. Eat a snack.

   B. Do a quiet activity.

   C. Do a little exercise.

   D. Play a game.

Reading Literature

3. What can happen if you do **not** get enough sleep?

   A. You may feel tired and happy.

   B. You may feel grumpy and curious.

   C. You may feel tired and grumpy.

   D. You may feel silly and sleepy.

4. According to the author, which of the following statements is true?

   A. Many children fall asleep in school.

   B. Many children go to sleep too early.

   C. Many children don't get enough sleep.

   D. Many children sleep late on weekends.

5. Which of the following expresses the author's feelings?

   A. It's important to sleep late.

   B. It's important to get enough sleep.

   C. It's important to take naps.

   D. It's important to read before going to sleep.

Write It Out Use the passage to help you write an answer to the question below.

6. Tell about a time that you didn't get enough sleep. Explain how you felt differently or acted differently. Also explain why or why not you think it is important to get enough sleep.

_____

_____

_____

Reading Literature

LESSON
18   Plot

WORDS TO
KNOW

Plot   what happens in a story, including all the events from the beginning to the middle to the end

---

Review It!   Read this paragraph. Use the Hint to help you understand the plot.

Meg walked out of school and over to the bike rack. Her bike was gone! The lock was on the ground. She knew it had been stolen. "Back to taking the bus," thought Meg.

> **Hint**   Often, the plot of a story includes a problem that has to be solved. Think about Meg's problem and how she solved it.

Try It!   Read this passage. As you read, <u>underline</u> sentences that tell about the problem and how it was solved.

(1) It was snowing hard, and Rick was walking home from his friend's house.
(2) Although it was only four blocks, the snow was rapidly turning into a
(3) blizzard. Rick glanced around and couldn't identify anything familiar in
(4) his neighborhood. Everything was totally white, and he felt confused and
(5) frightened! Then Rick noticed a red cap lying in the snow. He picked it up
(6) and broke off a branch that was hanging from a tree. Then he put the cap
(7) on the end of the branch and held it up high. If someone passed him, they
(8) would see his cap. Soon Mom's van pulled up alongside him. "I saw the
(9) red spot in the snow," she said. "You are a clever boy!"

Now, use the passage to answer the questions on the following page.

1. On lines 3–4, the heavy snow gave Rick problems because it made everything look

    A. cold and frosty   **C.** calm and peaceful

    B. clean and fresh   **D.** the same

2. What did Rick do to solve his problem?

    A. He put on a red cap to stay warm.

    B. He held up a branch with a red cap on the end.

    C. He used a branch to help him walk.

    D. He called his mom to pick him up.

3. Which word can be used to describe how Rick felt in the story?

    A. angry   **C.** scared

    B. amused   **D.** clever

4. Which of the following did **not** help Rick solve his problem?

    A. his mom

    B. the snow

    C. the red cap

    D. the branch

In Your Own Words

5. Why did Rick's mom call him a clever boy?

_____

_____

_____

Ask Yourself

1. Why couldn't Rick find anything familiar in his neighborhood?

3. Which word means the same as frightened?

5. What did Rick do to solve his problem?

Reading Literature

Read this passage. Answer the questions that follow it.

Reading Literature

Stanley was a contented squirrel that lived in an enormous oak tree in the Jensens' backyard. He had created a comfortable home in the old oak and hoped to spend his life there. At least, that was his plan until the Jensens brought home a large, spotted dog. After that, life for Stanley became quite miserable.

When he ran down from his nest, the dog barked and chased him. Since Stanley stored his food in the ground, this was a daily problem. Each time he went to his storage space, the spotted creature growled and chased him away.

Stanley was no longer contented. After giving it much thought, he decided he had to move. Moving was difficult for a squirrel Stanley's age, but he had no choice. As Stanley began packing, he heard loud noises below. When he looked down, he saw movers loading the Jensens' furniture into a van. The Jensens were moving! That meant Stanley could stay! Stanley hoped the family that moved in wouldn't have a dog. His wish came true. The new family had two cats—house cats.

1. How did Stanley feel at the beginning of the story?

   A. happy

   B. sad

   C. angry

   D. nervous

2. What was Stanley's problem?

   A. The Jensens were bad neighbors.

   B. The Jensens' dog ate his food.

   C. The Jensens' dog chased him.

   D. The Jensens' dog was lazy.

3. How did Stanley plan to solve his problem?

    A. He planned to make friends with the dog.

    B. He planned to speak to the Jensens.

    C. He planned to stay in his tree.

    D. He planned to move.

4. How did Stanley's problem get solved?

    A. The Jensens gave away the dog.

    B. Stanley moved away.

    C. The Jensens moved away.

    D. The dog ran away.

5. Why was Stanley happy about the new family that moved in?

    A. They looked friendly.

    B. They had two house cats.

    C. They had no pets.

    D. They had a small dog.

Write It Out   Use the passage to help you write an answer to the question below.

6. Think about some other good solutions to Stanley's problem. Write about **one** solution on the lines below.

_____

_____

_____

_____

Reading Literature

LESSON

19 Character

WORDS TO
KNOW
Character a person or an animal that is in a story. Readers find out about characters by noticing what they say and do.

Review It! Read this paragraph. Use the Hint to help you understand the character in the story.

Richard is a firefighter. Last week he ran into a burning building and rescued three young children. Then he put out the fire. Later, Richard said, "I was only doing my job."

Hint Think about what Richard did and said in order to figure out his character.

Try It! Read this passage. As you read, circle the names of the two characters. Then underline words and sentences that show you what the characters are like.

(1)   Once upon a time, a crow noticed a piece of cheese on the ground.
(2)   He was delighted to discover the cheese and thought it would make a
(3)   delicious meal. The crow picked up the cheese with his beak and flew
(4)   to a nearby branch to eat it. Just at that moment, a fox came strolling by.
(5)   The fox wanted the cheese, so he began complimenting the crow. "I've
(6)   heard that you sing beautifully!" said the fox. "Won't you sing for me?"
(7)   The crow wanted to show off his beautiful voice and began to sing. The
(8)   cheese then fell to the ground, and the fox ran away with it.

Now, use the passage to answer the questions on the following page.

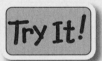

Reading Literature

1. Which of the following **best** describes the fox?

   A. shy and kind   **C.** smart and helpful

   B. sly and selfish   **D.** sad and brave

2. What did you learn about the crow on lines 7–8?

   A. The crow is dishonest.

   B. The crow is very clever.

   C. The crow is proud of his voice.

   D. The crow is very shy.

3. Which word describes how the crow probably felt at the end of the story?

   A. happy   **C.** scared

   B. calm   **D.** foolish

4. Which sentence would **not** describe how the fox probably felt at the end of the story?

   A. The fox felt disappointed.

   B. The fox felt happy.

   C. The fox felt satisfied.

   D. The fox felt excited.

In Your Own Words

5. Pretend you are the crow, and tell how you feel about the fox.

_____

_____

_____

1.
How did the fox act toward the crow?

2.
Why did the crow sing?

5.
What did the fox do to the crow?

Reading Literature

Read this passage. Answer the questions that follow it.

Jose needed to make some money over the summer. He wanted to buy sneakers and a jacket for the next school year. He knew he would have to work for it, but he was willing. He walked around the neighborhood asking people if they needed help with anything. Finally, Mr. Young, the owner of the corner store, agreed to pay Jose to help him close the store every night at 6:00. Mr. Young would pay him $5 a day, Monday to Saturday. Jose was excited. He was going to be making $30 every week. Mr. Young was a nice man, too. All the kids liked him.

On his first day, Jose played basketball with his friends all afternoon, but left the courts early so he wouldn't be late for Mr. Young. When Jose arrived, Mr. Young carefully showed him what needed to be done. Jose knew he could handle it.

Jose spent the whole summer hanging out with his friends during the day and helping Mr. Young at exactly 6:00 every night. Mr. Young grew to trust Jose and gave him other jobs, like stocking the shelves and arranging the new products. Mr. Young even gave Jose a $1 raise in July. By mid-August, Jose had saved up enough for sneakers, a jacket, and some t-shirts.

1. Why did Jose work over his summer vacation?

   A. He wanted something to do.

   B. He wanted to earn money.

   C. He didn't have friends.

   D. He was bored.

2. Mr. Young is

   A. impatient and mean

   B. shy and weak

   C. wise and well-liked

   D. cold and distant

Reading Literature

3. By being on time every day, Jose showed that he

   A. was responsible

   B. only wanted to play basketball

   C. didn't care about his job

   D. had better things to do

4. Mr. Young showed that he thought Jose was a good worker by

   A. asking him to stop coming in

   B. reminding him to be on time

   C. ignoring him

   D. giving him a raise

5. How did Jose probably feel at the end of the summer?

   A. worried

   B. tired

   C. sad

   D. happy

Write It Out   Use the passage to help you write an answer to the question below.

6. Jose will probably want a job for next summer. List **three** reasons why Mr. Young should hire Jose, again.

   _____

   _____

   _____

   _____

WORDS TO KNOW **Setting** where and when a story takes place

 Read this paragraph. Use the Hint to help you identify the setting.

Dad was cooking breakfast when Kim walked into the room. He smiled as Kim placed Mom's birthday card on her plate. Kim hoped Mom would like what she had written.

> **Hint** Think about the fact that Dad was cooking breakfast. That will help you identify the setting.

 Read this passage. As you read, <u>underline</u> words and sentences that tell you about the setting.

(1) Mom and Dad were putting up the tent while Jane and I unpacked our
(2) camping gear. The air smelled so fresh that we all took several deep breaths.
(3) After setting things up, we spent the afternoon hiking on the beautiful
(4) grounds and then swimming in the blue lake. Mom said that it was a
(5) pleasant change to be away from cell phones and computers. At night, we
(6) cooked dinner over a crackling campfire and then turned in early. From the
(7) tent, I peeked out and saw a night sky that was filled with twinkling stars.

Now, use the passage to answer the questions on the following page.

1. Where does the story take place?

   A. in a city

   B. on a ranch

   C. on a farm

   D. in a campground

Ask Yourself

1.
What details tell you the setting?

2. Which of the following is part of the story's setting?

   A. lake   **C.** computer

   B. Jane   **D.** cell phone

3. What time of day is being described at the end of the story?

   A. morning   **C.** night

   B. noon   **D.** dawn

4. By reading lines 4–5, you know that the story takes place

   A. about 50 years ago

   B. in the 1800s

   C. in the present

   D. more than 50 years ago

4.
What do the words *cell phones* and *computers* tell you?

In Your Own Words

5. Write about something else you might see in the setting from the story.

_____

_____

_____

5.
What kinds of animals or landscapes might you see in this setting?

Reading Literature

On Your Own!

Read this passage. Answer the questions that follow it.

Jack loved this time of year. School was out and the weather was terrific. Plus, his favorite spot was opening for the season. He couldn't wait to jump into the cool water. Jack and his friend Harry were the first ones at the gate.

The minute Jack put down his towel, he ran to the diving board. He was running quickly and the concrete was slippery. He skidded and fell on his back. Pam, the lifeguard, was there in seconds. "Are you alright?" she asked. Harry was concerned, too. Jack nodded that he was fine. His knee was scraped a bit. Pam reminded Jack about the "no running" rule. Jack apologized and said it wouldn't happen again. The boys got back into the water. As Jack swam, he decided that he didn't need to rush. He had three months of long, hot days to enjoy the pool.

After lunch, Jack and Harry were at a table when Pam came by. Jack looked down because he still felt ashamed. Surprisingly, Pam paid them a compliment. "I've been watching you, and you're both excellent swimmers!" Jack and Harry both grinned, and Jack felt good again.

1. The setting of this story is
   A. the beach
   B. a lake
   C. a pool
   D. a park

2. When does the story **most likely** take place?
   A. in winter
   B. in spring
   C. in summer
   D. in fall

3. What detail tells you the boys have arrived at the pool?

   A. They are the first ones at the gate.

   B. Jack sets down his towel.

   C. Pam runs over when Jack slips.

   D. The concrete was slippery.

4. Jack and Harry enjoy the pool because

   A. it is the best place to meet

   B. it cools them off

   C. it is the only place to go

   D. it is a great place in the winter

5. Which of the following is part of the story's setting?

   A. Jack

   B. lunch

   C. clothes

   D. diving board

Write It Out Use the passage to help you write an answer to the question below.

6. Imagine that Jack and Harry lived near the beach. Write at least **three** details from a day at the beach. Think about where they swim, where they rest, and how the rules are different.

_____

_____

_____

_____

Reading Literature

WORDS TO KNOW **Theme** the message or the general meaning of a story

---

Review It! Read this paragraph. Use the Hint to help you identify the theme.

Cara practiced the tap dancing routine all morning, but she just couldn't get it. Cara continued to practice. By the end of the day, she had it!

Hint Think about how Cara kept trying. That will help you identify the message, or theme.

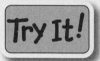 **Try It!** Read this passage. As you read, <u>underline</u> words and sentences that tell about the message, or theme.

(1) One day, a thirsty ant was taking a drink of water from the river.

(2) Unfortunately, the ant fell in and was carried along by the rushing current.

(3) A dove noticed that the ant was in trouble and threw a leaf into the water.

(4) The ant crawled onto the leaf and made it safely to the riverbank, where he

(5) thanked the dove for saving his life. Several days later, the ant saw a hunter

(6) aiming his arrow at the dove. The ant crawled on the hunter's foot and bit

(7) him as hard as possible! The hunter then dropped his arrow and the dove's

(8) life was spared.

Now, use the passage to answer the questions on the following page.

1. On lines 3–4, you find out that

   A. the dove helps the ant **C.** the ant hurts the hunter

   B. the ant helps the dove **D.** the hunter hurts the dove

2. How does the ant save the dove's life?

   A. The ant tosses a leaf.

   B. The ant jumps in the river.

   C. The ant bites the hunter.

   D. The ant shouts at the dove.

2.
Why does the hunter drop his arrow?

3. Which of the following **best** describes this story's subject?

   A. courage   **C.** teaching others.

   B. helping others   **D.** helping family

3.
What does the dove do for the ant? What does the ant do for the dove?

4. What is the message of the story?

   A. If you are greedy, then you will end up with nothing.

   B. If you work hard, then you will succeed.

   C. If you help others, then others will help you.

   D. If you think about a problem, then you will solve it.

In Your Own Words

5. What other story have you read that has a similar theme? What happens in the story? Write **two** or **three** sentences of your own about the story.

5.
How do the story's characters help each other?

_____

_____

_____

_____

Reading Literature

Read this passage. Answer the questions that follow it.

Long ago, there lived an ant and a grasshopper. The ant was a hard worker, and each summer morning, he woke up early to gather food for winter. The grasshopper, on the other hand, couldn't be bothered with work. Each morning, he slept late and spent the day amusing himself in a variety of ways.

Frequently, the grasshopper asked the ant to play with him. However, the ant always refused, explaining that he had to gather food for winter. The grasshopper made fun of the ant, saying he was foolish to worry about winter on a beautiful summer day!

When fall came, the ant worked even harder. The grasshopper, however, continued to play all day. Soon winter arrived with a blizzard. The ant relaxed in his cozy home. He wasn't worried because he had enough food. The grasshopper, however, was cold and hungry. So he went to the ant's house to ask for food. "I'm sorry," said the ant. "I don't have enough food for both of us." Then he added, "You spent the summer playing and made fun of me for working hard. I hope you have learned a lesson."

1. The ant and the grasshopper can **best** be described as

   A. similar

   B. friendly

   C. interesting

   D. opposites

2. Which of the following **best** describes the ant?

   A. He likes winter.

   B. He doesn't rest.

   C. He plans ahead.

   D. He is greedy.

Reading Literature

3. Which of the following **best** describes the grasshopper?

   A. He is smart and happy.

   B. He is hard working and careful.

   C. He is polite and respectful.

   D. He is foolish and lazy.

4. What is the **theme** of the story?

   A. It is important to have a good time.

   B. It is important to prepare for the future.

   C. It is important to have a friend.

   D. It is important to wake up early.

5. According to this story, if you don't prepare for the future

   A. you will suffer

   B. you will live in the past

   C. you will be alone

   D. you will be cold

Write It Out Use the story to help you write a brief answer to the question below.

6. How can the message of this story be applied to everyday life?

   _____

   _____

Reading Literature

Reading Literature

WORDS TO KNOW   **Summarizing**   giving the main idea and important details of the text in your own words

---

Review It!   Read this paragraph. Use the Hint to help you summarize it.

My friends and I go to the neighborhood community center after school. It has a computer room. There are basketball and tennis courts. There is also an art room where we can do all kinds of crafts.

Hint Think about what the kids do at the community center. That will help you summarize the paragraph.

Try It!   Read this passage. As you read, <u>underline</u> sentences that tell the main idea and give important details.

(1) Most plants require seeds in order to create new plants. Often, these seeds
(2) are better able to grow when they move away from the parent plant.
(3) Seeds can travel from one location to another in a variety of ways. Some
(4) seeds, such as those of the dandelion, travel by wind. These seeds are light
(5) enough for the wind to carry them to new places. Other seeds use animals
(6) to assist them in traveling to new locations. Animals, such as the bison,
(7) carry numerous seeds on their fur. Still other seeds travel by floating on
(8) water. Rivers and oceans can move seeds like those of the coconut palm
(9) to new places.

Now, use the passage to answer the questions on the following page.

1. This passage is about

    A. how seeds taste   **C.** how seeds grow

    B. how seeds look   **D.** how seeds travel

2. Which sentence below belongs in a summary of the passage?

    A. Some trees have seeds.

    B. Some seeds travel on water.

    C. Some animals eat seeds.

    D. Some seeds are small.

2.
Which detail is about seeds going from place to place?

3. Which sentence does **not** belong in a summary of the passage?

    A. Animals carry seeds.

    B. Seeds travel by wind.

    C. Seeds travel on water.

    D. Coconut palm trees have seeds.

4. How many ways do seeds travel, according to the passage?

    A. one   **C.** three

    B. two   **D.** four

4.
Can you find the examples of traveling seeds in the passage?

In Your Own Words

5. Summarize the passage in your own words.

    _____

    _____

    _____

    _____

5.
What is the **main** idea? What are the important details? How can you tell about them in your own words?

Reading Literature

On Your Own!

Read this passage. Answer the questions that follow it.

The cactus is especially well-suited to live in the desert. In a place where there is little rain, the cactus can store water in its thick, hard-walled stem. A thick, waxy coating prevents the water inside the cactus from evaporating.

A typical cactus has spines or scales instead of leaves. Like the stem, the spines and scales prevent the cactus from losing water. The spines also keep animals from munching on the cactus! Plants that have thin, flat leaves could never survive in such a hot, dry place. They lose water through their leaves too easily.

The roots of the cactus also help it survive in the desert. Cactus roots grow out to the side rather than straight down. Since the roots are close to the surface, they can soak up water from even the lightest rainfall. The roots of other plants grow deep in the soil and could never absorb enough water before it evaporated into the hot, dry soil and air.

1. Why is a cactus able to live in the desert?

   A. It can store water.
   B. Its roots grow down.
   C. It has large leaves.
   D. It can feed animals.

2. Which of the following is true about the cactus?

   A. It has thin, flat leaves.
   B. It has a yellowish color.
   C. It has a waxy coating.
   D. It has a thin stem.

3. Where does a cactus store water?

   A. in its stem

   B. in its scales

   C. in its skin

   D. in the sand

4. Which sentence belongs in a summary of the passage?

   A. A cactus is an interesting plant.

   B. A cactus is a green plant.

   C. A cactus soaks up water easily.

   D. A cactus can grow flowers.

5. Which sentence does **not** belong in a summary of the passage?

   A. A cactus can grow in very dry places.

   B. Spines and scales prevent the cactus from losing water.

   C. Cactus roots grow close to the surface.

   D. Some plants have roots that grow deep in the soil.

Write It Out   Use the passage to help you write a brief answer to the question below.

6. How would you summarize this passage?

_____

_____

_____

_____

Reading Literature

> WORDS TO **KNOW** | **Rhyme** the repeating sounds in words at the end of lines in a poem. **Rhythm** the number of beats or syllables in each line of a poem

 Review It! Read this poem. Use the Hint to help you figure out the rhyme and rhythm.

Twinkle, twinkle, little star,
How I wonder what you are!
Up above the world so high,
Like a diamond in the sky.

Hint Notice how each line of the poem ends to find the rhyming words. Count the number of syllables in each line to identify the rhythm.

Try It! Read this limerick. As you read, <u>underline</u> the rhyming words. Then count the syllables in each line.

1   There was an Old Man in a tree,
2   Who was horribly bored by a Bee;
3   When they said, "Does it buzz?"
4   He replied, "Yes it does!"
5   "It's a regular brute of a Bee!"

Edward Lear

Now, use the limerick to answer the questions on the following page.

Reading Literature

1. Which of the following words from the limerick rhyme?

    A. *tree* and *does*   **C.** *Bee* and *buzz*

    B. *buzz* and *does*   **D.** *buzz* and *brute*

2. Which of the following is true about the limerick?

    A. Lines 1, 2, and 5 rhyme.

    B. Lines 1, 3, and 5 rhyme.

    C. Lines 2 and 4 rhyme.

    D. Lines 3, 4, and 5 rhyme.

    > **2.**
    > Does the last word in each line end with the same sound?

3. Line 3 of the limerick has the same number of beats as

    A. line 1   **C.** line 4

    B. line 2   **D.** line 5

    > **3.**
    > How many syllables do you hear in each line?

4. How many beats does line 1 have?

    A. 6   **C.** 8

    B. 7   **D.** 9

In Your Own Words

5. What are **two** differences between the **two** poems on page 94?

    _____

    _____

    _____

    _____

    > **5.**
    > How many lines does each poem have? Which lines in each poem rhyme?

Reading Literature

Read this poem. Answer the questions that follow it.

The Cow

(1) The friendly cow all red and white,

(2) I love with all my heart:

(3) She gives me cream, with all her might,

(4) To eat with apple-tart.

(5) She wanders lowing here and there,

(6) And yet she cannot stray,

(7) All in the pleasant open air,

(8) The pleasant light of day;

(9) And blown by all the winds that pass

(10) And wet with all the showers,

(11) She walks among the meadow grass

(12) And eats the meadow flowers.

Robert Louis Stevenson

1. Which words from the poem rhyme?

    A. *there* and *air*

    B. *there* and *she*

    C. *there* and *the*

    D. *there* and *eat*

2. Which words from the poem do **not** rhyme?

    A. *heart* and *tart*

    B. *might* and *white*

    C. *flowers* and *showers*

    D. *flowers* and *blown*

Reading Literature

3. How many beats does the last line have?

    A. 5

    B. 6

    C. 7

    D. 8

4. Which two other lines in the poem have the same rhythm?

    A. lines 5 and 6

    B. lines 6 and 7

    C. lines 6 and 8

    D. lines 8 and 9

5. Line 1 of the poem has the same rhythm as

    A. line 2

    B. line 3

    C. line 4

    D. line 6

Write It Out Use the poem to help you answer the question below.

6. How many pairs of rhyming words can you find in the poem? Write them on the lines.

    _____

    _____

    _____

LESSON 24 Types of Sentences

WORDS TO KNOW **Sentence** a complete thought. **Declarative sentences** sentences that make statements. **Imperative sentences** sentences that give orders. **Interrogative sentences** sentences that ask questions. **Exclamatory sentences** sentences that exclaim with excitement.

 Read this paragraph. Use the Hint to help you identify the different types of sentences.

Do you wear a helmet when you go skating or biking? I certainly hope so! A helmet protects your head and brain from injury. So please don't take chances with your safety.

Hint Look at the end punctuation to help you identify different types of sentences. For a sentence that ends with a period, think about whether it tells or commands.

 Read this passage. As you read, <u>underline</u> and label the four types of sentences.

(1) Every four years, without fail, Americans vote for the person they want
(2) to be president of our country. People go out to vote on Election Day,
(3) which is always the first Tuesday in November. Who is eligible to vote?
(4) Citizens who are at least 18 years of age can register to vote. Do you
(5) know that some people don't bother to vote? What a shame that is, since
(6) voting is one of the most important things a citizen can do! If you are 18
(7) or older, go out and vote.

Now, use the passage to answer the questions on the following page.

1. The first sentence in the passage is

   A. declarative   **C.** interrogative

   B. imperative   **D.** exclamatory

2. The sentence on lines 4 and 5 is

   A. a declarative sentence

   B. an imperative sentence

   C. an interrogative sentence

   D. an exclamatory sentence

3. How many interrogative sentences are in the passage?

   A. one   **C.** three

   B. two   **D.** four

4. The last sentence in the passage is

   A. declarative

   B. imperative

   C. interrogative

   D. exclamatory

In Your Own Words

5. Write **two** sentences that give your opinion about citizenship. Make the sentences different types.

   _____

   _____

   _____

   _____

Ask Yourself

1.
How does the sentence end? Does the sentence tell or command?

3.
How many sentences ask questions? How do these sentences end?

5.
Do the sentences tell, command, ask, or show strong feeling?

Writing, Editing, Mechanics

Read this passage. Answer the questions that follow it.

Have you ever heard someone call a koala a *koala bear?* Perhaps it's because koalas resemble adorable teddy bears! However, they aren't members of the bear family at all. Koalas are actually members of a group of animals called *marsupials*. A marsupial is an animal that has a pouch for carrying its young. Many kinds of marsupials, such as koalas and kangaroos, live in Australia.

A mother koala gives birth to one baby a year. The newborn koala is called a *joey*. A joey is about as big as a large jelly bean! At first, it stays in its mother's pouch and drinks her milk. However, after a few months, it leaves the pouch and climbs on its mother's back. What do koalas eat? They love to eat the leaves of eucalyptus trees.

People are frequently tempted to reach out and touch koalas because they look so cute and cuddly. However, doing that is quite dangerous. Do not try to pet koalas. They are wild animals that have extremely sharp claws. Koalas also have strong arm and shoulder muscles that help them climb and jump from tree to tree.

---

1. The first sentence in the passage is
   - **A.** declarative
   - **B.** imperative
   - **C.** interrogative
   - **D.** exclamatory

2. The last sentence in the passage is
   - **A.** declarative
   - **B.** imperative
   - **C.** interrogative
   - **D.** exclamatory

3. How many exclamatory sentences are in the passage?

  A. one

  B. two

  C. three

  D. four

4. Which of the following sentences from the passage is imperative?

  A. The newborn koala is called a *joey*.

  B. They enjoy eating the leaves of eucalyptus trees.

  C. Do not try to pet koalas.

  D. They are wild animals that have long, sharp claws.

5. Which of the following is true about the passage?

  A. There are more imperative than declarative sentences.

  B. There are more interrogative than declarative sentences.

  C. There are more exclamatory than interrogative sentences.

  D. There are more declarative than interrogative sentences.

Write It Out Use the passage to answer the question below.

6. How many sentences of each type are there in the passage?

_____

_____

_____

LESSON 25 Punctuation

WORDS TO KNOW **punctuation** marks within a text that help readers better understand its meaning. A **period** ends a statement. A **question mark** signals a question. An **exclamation point** signals excitement. A **comma** separates cities and states, days and years, and words in a series.

 **Read the paragraph. Use the Hint to help you identify the different types of punctuation.**

Happy birthday to America! Our country claimed its independence from England on July 4, 1776. Today we celebrate with parades, fireworks, and picnics. How do you celebrate our country's birthday?

Hint Look at the punctuation at the end of each sentence. Notice the way commas are used.

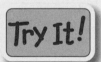 **Read this passage. As you read, <u>underline</u> places where end punctuation or commas are missing.**

(1) Rosa Parks has been called heroic strong and steadfast. Do you know
(2) why? She did something amazing on December 1, 1955. It happened
(3) in the African-American community of Montgomery, Alabama. Rosa
(4) Parks was riding a city bus. The bus driver told her to give her seat to a
(5) white passenger. When Rosa Parks refused, she was arrested! After that,
(6) thousands of people stopped riding buses in Montgomery. What happened
(7) next The United States Supreme Court ruled that segregated buses were
(8) illegal on November 13 1956. Rosa Parks won!

Now, use the passage to answer the questions on the following page.

1. **What do you call the punctuation at the end of the last sentence?**

   A. comma   **C.** period

   B. exclamation point   **D.** question mark

2. **Which punctuation mark belongs at the end of the sentence on line 7?**

   A. .   **C.** !

   B. ?   **D.** ,

> **2.** Does the sentence ask or tell?

3. **Which shows the date on lines 7 and 8 written correctly?**

   A. November 13 1956   **C.** November 13, 1956

   B. November, 13, 1956   **D.** November 13 1,956

4. **Which shows the first sentence of the passage written correctly?**

   A. Rosa Parks has been called heroic strong, and steadfast.

   B. Rosa Parks has been called heroic strong and steadfast.

   C. Rosa Parks has been called heroic, strong, and steadfast,

   D. Rosa Parks has been called heroic, strong, and steadfast.

> **4.** How do you separate words in a series?

In Your Own Words

5. **Make up your own last sentence for the passage. End your sentence with correct punctuation.**

_____

_____

_____

> **5.** Does your sentence ask, tell, or show excitement?

Writing, Editing, Mechanics

Ben Franklin was a man of many achievements. He was an inventor, a printer, and a writer. He was also a founder of our country. Ben was born in Boston Massachusetts, on January 17 1706. Believe it or not, he attended school for only two years! Why? His family was poor and he needed to work.

Even so, Ben loved books. Sometimes he went hungry in order to buy a book! At 12, Ben started working in his brother's printing shop. However, when the two brothers didn't get along, Ben ran away. Where did he go First he went to New York. Then he settled in Philadelphia Pennsylvania. Ben opened his own printing shop there. He started a newspaper and wrote an almanac.

Ben loved Philadelphia and worked hard to make it a good place to live. He set up the first fire department hospital and library. He also invented a variety of things. His inventions included the lightning rod, the Franklin Stove, and eyeglasses. Later on, Ben helped write the Declaration of Independence and the U.S. Constitution. Ben Franklin died on April 17, 1790 at the age of 84. He was a truly remarkable man!

---

1. How many sentences end with an exclamation point?

    A. one

    B. two

    C. three

    D. four

2. Which shows the city and state written correctly?

    A. Philadelphia – Pennsylvania

    B. Philadelphia, Pennsylvania

    C. Philadelphia. Pennsylvania

    D. Philadelphia Pennsylvania

3. Which of the following sentences is written correctly?

    A. Where did he go.

    B. Where did he go!

    C. Where did he go,

    D. Where did he go?

4. Which of the following sentences is written correctly?

    A. He set up the first fire department, hospital, and library.

    B. He set up the first fire, department, hospital and library.

    C. He set up the first fire department hospital, and library.

    D. He set up the first fire department hospital and library.

5. Which of the following sentences is written correctly?

    A. Ben was born in Boston Massachusetts, on January 17 1706.

    B. Ben was born in Boston, Massachusetts, on January 17 1706.

    C. Ben was born in Boston Massachusetts, on January 17, 1706.

    D. Ben was born in Boston, Massachusetts, on January 17, 1706.

Write It Out   Use the passage to help you write a brief answer to the question below.

6. If you could interview Ben Franklin today, what question would you ask him? What would his answer be? Write the **two** sentences with correct punctuation.

_____

_____

_____

_____

LESSON 26 Capitalization

WORDS TO KNOW   **Capital letters** should be used at the beginning of the first word in a sentence. They should also begin names of people, places, and things.

 **Review It!**   Read the paragraph. Use the Hint to help you identify how capital letters are used.

Mark Twain is one of America's most famous writers. His real name was Samuel Clemens, and he was born in Hannibal, Missouri, in 1835.

Hint Notice the different names in the paragraph. Also look at the way each sentence begins.

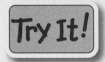 **Try It!**   Read this passage. As you read, <u>underline</u> words that should begin with a capital letter.

(1) Clara barton was born in oxford, massachusetts. She taught school and
(2) worked at the United States Patent Office. when the civil war broke out,
(3) clara worked as a nurse. She brought supplies to soldiers and worked on
(4) the battlefield. In fact, she was called the "angel of the battlefield." in
(5) 1869, clara went to europe. There she worked with the International
(6) red Cross. Clara returned to the U.S. in 1873. In 1881, she set up the
(7) American National Red Cross. Clara Barton helped many people during
(8) her lifetime.

Now, use the passage to answer the questions on the following page.

Writing, Editing, Mechanics

Ask Yourself

1. Which words should be capitalized in the sentence on lines 2–3?

   A. When, Civil, Clara   **C.** When, Civil War, Clara

   B. When, Civil War   **D.** When, Clara, Nurse

1.
When should you use capital letters?

2. Which shows the sentence on lines 4–5 written correctly?

   A. in 1869, Clara went to Europe.

   B. In 1869, Clara went to Europe.

   C. In 1869, clara went to Europe.

   D. In 1869, Clara went to europe.

3. Which of the following is written correctly?

   A. international red cross **C.** International Red Cross

   B. International Red cross **D.** International red Cross

4. Which shows the first sentence of the passage written correctly?

   A. Clara Barton was born in oxford, massachusetts.

   B. Clara barton was born in Oxford, Massachusetts.

   C. Clara Barton was born in oxford, Massachusetts.

   D. Clara Barton was born in Oxford, Massachusetts.

4.
What kinds of names get capitalized?

In Your Own Words

5. Make up your own sentence about Clara Barton and the good work she did. Use correct capitalization.

_____

_____

_____

5.
How should a person's name be written? How should a sentence start?

Writing, Editing, Mechanics

Read this passage. Answer the questions that follow it.

In 1860, a mail service called the Pony Express was created. the Pony Express riders rode on horseback across the western part of the united states to deliver mail. people in california were able to get mail from people in missouri in only ten days!

A man named william hepburn russell came up with the idea of the pony express. Before that, the quickest way to deliver mail was by stagecoach. stagecoaches went from missouri to texas and then on to california. The trip took about 25 days.

Right away, the Pony Express was a success! The young men who became riders were admired by all. one of the most famous riders was bill cody. He later became known as Buffalo Bill! So why did the Pony Express last only a year and a half? The invention of the telegraph by Samuel Morse changed everything. People could send messages by wire in seconds, and the Pony Express was no longer needed.

---

1. Which words should be capitalized in the **second** sentence of the passage?

   A. The, United States

   B. The, Horseback, Western

   C. The, Western, States

   D. Horseback, United States,

2. Which words should be capitalized in the **third** sentence of the passage?

   A. California, Mail, Missouri

   B. People, Mail, Missouri

   C. People, California, Missouri

   D. California, Able, Missouri

3. Which words should be capitalized in the **fourth** sentence of the passage?

A. William Russell, Idea, Pony Express

B. William Hepburn Russell, Pony Express

C. William Hepburn Russell, Up, Pony

D. William Hepburn Russell, Idea, Express

4. Which of the following sentences is written correctly?

A. one of the most famous riders was bill cody.

B. One of the most famous riders was bill cody.

C. One of the most famous riders was Bill cody.

D. One of the most famous riders was Bill Cody.

5. Which words should be capitalized in the **sixth** sentence of the passage?

A. Went, Missouri, Texas, Then

B. Stagecoaches, Went, Texas, California

C. Stagecoaches, Missouri, Texas, California

D. Stagecoaches, Missouri, Then, California

Write It Out Use the passage to help you write a brief answer to the question below.

6. What would have been the **best** part about being a Pony Express rider? What would have been the **worst** part? Use correct capitalization in your sentences.

_____

_____

_____

_____

LESSON 27 Spelling

WORDS TO KNOW **Spelling** a group of letters that together represent a word. In English, many words follow the same spelling patterns and rules.

Review It! Read the paragraph. Use the Hint to see how to spell the underlined words correctly.

How often do you brush your teeth? Brush them after <u>evry</u> meal and before you go to <u>slep</u> at night. Take your time and don't brush <u>qickly</u>.

> **Hint** The correct spellings for the underlined words are *every*, *sleep*, and *quickly*.

Try It! Read this passage. As you read, <u>underline</u> words that are not spelled correctly.

1. Health experts beleive that people are eating too much junk food today.
2. They also think that it's importint for people to develop healthy eating
3. habits at a young age. What foods should we includ in our diet? We
4. should eat fruits, vegetables, and whole grains, such as whole-wheat bread
5. and brown rice. We should also eat foods with calcium, such as milc,
6. yogurd, and cheese. What foods should we avoid? We shouldn't eat junk
7. food, such as potato chips and candy bars. Junk food contains too much fat
8. and sugar.

Now, use the passage to answer the questions on the following page.

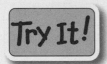

1. Which word is misspelled on line 1 of the passage?

   A. experts   **C.** beleive

   B. eating   **D.** junk

2. What is the correct spelling of *importint* on line 2 of the passage?

   A. improtint

   B. impertent

   C. importunt

   D. important

3. Which word is misspelled on line 3 of the passage?

   A. habits   **C.** includ

   B. young   **D.** diet

4. Which **two** words are misspelled on line 5 of the passage?

   A. milc and cheese

   B. milc and yogurd

   C. yogurd and cheese

   D. milc and avoid

In Your Own Words

5. Write a sentence about what a healthy snack would be. Check your spelling.

_____

_____

_____

Ask Yourself

1. What is the spelling pattern for words that have *i* and *e*?

4. What sound do you hear at the end of each word? What letter stands for each sound?

5. How can sounding out words help you spell them correctly?

Read this passage. Answer the questions that follow it.

Recent studies have foud that American childen are carrying backpacks that are too heavy. Kids should carry fewer things so that they lighten their backpack load. Why? A heavy backpack can cause back and shoulder pain. Over time, this can leed to serious back and shoulder problems. Another finding was that uneven backpack loads can cause pain in the lower back.

Health experts say that a nine-year-old's backpack should not weigh more that eight pounds. One study found that some kids were actually carrying more than twalve pounds in their backpacks. That is much too heavy!

Another suggestion was that shoulder straps on backpacks should be wide and well-paded. They should also be adjusted for a snug fit. So please make sure that you follow the backpack safety rules. If you do, you'll avod back and shouder problems later on!

1. **Which words are misspelled in the first sentence of paragraph 1?**

   A. studies and foud

   B. foud and American

   C. American and childen

   D. foud and childen

2. **Which word is misspelled in the fifth sentence of paragraph 1?**

   A. over

   B. serious

   C. shoulder

   D. leed

3. What is the correct spelling of *twalve* in paragraph 2?

   A. twelv

   B. twalv

   C. twelve

   D. twevle

4. Which word is misspelled in the first sentence of paragraph 3?

   A. shoulder

   B. suggestion

   C. well-paded

   D. should

5. Which **two** words are misspelled in the last sentence of the passage?

   A. you'll and avod

   B. avod and shouder

   C. shouder and problems

   D. shouder and later

Write It Out Use the passage to help you write a brief answer to the question below.

6. What things do you bring to school each day? Are you following the backpack safety rules? Check for correct spelling in your sentences.

   _____

   _____

   _____

LESSON 28 Subject-Verb Agreement

WORDS TO KNOW

Subject person, place, or thing in a sentence doing an action. The **verb** is an action word in a sentence. **Subject-verb agreement** means that the form of a noun should match the form of a verb.

Review It! Read the sentences. Use the Hint to identify the singular and plural subjects and verbs.

A hurricane spins wild winds.
Hurricanes form over oceans.

> **Hint** Notice that the first sentence has a singular subject and the verb ends with *s*. The second sentence has a plural subject and the verb does not end with *s*.

Try It! Read this passage. As you read, <u>underline</u> words that are subjects and verbs.

(1) Most people stops to admire a rainbow. However, most people don't
(2) understand what a rainbow is. So let's read on to find out! After a
(3) rainstorm, tiny raindrops stay in the air. The cloud pass and the suns come
(4) out. Sunlight look colorless or white most of the time. But sunlight is
(5) actually made up of seven colors: red, orange, yellow, green, blue, indigo,
(6) and violet. The colors is always there. However, we only see them when
(7) sunlight shines through the raindrops. Then the light separates into its
(8) seven colors. Then we see a beautiful rainbow!

Now, use the passage to answer the questions on the following page.

Writing, Editing, Mechanics

114

1. How should the subject and verb in the first sentence be written?

    A. peoples stops   **C.** people stop

    B. people stops   **D.** peoples stop

2. Which shows the sentence on lines 3–4 written correctly?

    A. The clouds pass and the sun comes out.

    B. The clouds passes and the sun come out.

    C. The cloud pass and the sun come out.

    D. The clouds pass and the suns come out.

3. How should the subject and verb on line 4 be written?

    A. Sunlights looked   **C.** Sunlight looks

    B. Sunlight look   **D.** Sunlights looks

4. Which shows the sentence on line 6 written correctly?

    A. The colors is always there.

    B. The color are always there.

    C. The colors am always there.

    D. The colors are always there.

In Your Own Words

5. What do you think about when you see a rainbow? Write a sentence about it. Make sure the subject and the verb agree.

_____

_____

_____

Ask Yourself

1. Are the subject and verb plural? What is the correct form of the verb?

2. Which noun is singular? Which noun is plural? Does the verb agree with each noun?

5. What is the subject of your sentence? Does the verb agree with the subject?

Writing, Editing, Mechanics

On Your Own!

Read this passage. Answer the questions that follow it.

Ants is such interesting insects! They are constantly busy, and they are extremely hard workers. Ants lives in groups called colonies. Some large colonies contain millions of ants.

Four different types of ants live in a colony. Each type have a different job. The queen ant lays the eggs. She are usually larger than the other ants. Typically, there is only one queen ant in a colony. A colony have only a few male ants. Male ants and the queen ant create baby ants. Worker ants builds the nest and searches for food. They also take care of the baby ants. Soldier ants protect the other members of the colony. Both worker ants and soldier ants are females.

Ants are found practically everywhere on earth. So is the stories about them! Because they are such fascinating creatures, ants are often used as story characters in many cultures of the world.

1. How should the subject and verb in the first sentence be written?

   A. Ants am
   B. Ant is
   C. Ants are
   D. Ant are

2. Which of the following sentences is written correctly?

   A. Ant live in groups called colonies.
   B. Ants live in groups called colonies.
   C. Ants lives in groups called colonies.
   D. Ant living in groups called colonies.

3. Which of the following sentences is written correctly?

   A. She am usually larger than the other ants.

   B. She are usually larger than the other ants.

   C. She were usually larger than the other ants.

   D. She is usually larger than the other ants.

4. Which of the following sentences is written correctly?

   A. A colony have only a few male ants.

   B. A colony haves only a few male ants.

   C. A colony has only a few male ants.

   D. A colony are only a few male ants.

5. Which of the following sentences is written correctly?

   A. Worker ants build the nest and search for food.

   B. Worker ants builds the nest and searches for food.

   C. Worker ants build the nest and searches for food.

   D. Worker ants builds the nest and search for food.

Write It Out   Use the passage to help you answer the question below.

6. Read the last paragraph of the passage. In which sentence does the verb **not** agree with the subject? Rewrite the sentence correctly.

   _____

   _____

Words to Know

Author's perspective what an author feels and believes about a topic. Sometimes an author's perspective shows **bias**, a strong feeling that affects the writer's opinion. (Page 62)

Author's purpose the reason an author writes something. An author may write to entertain, give information, explain how to do something, or express an opinion. (Page 70)

C

Capital letters should be used at the beginning of the first word in a sentence. They should also be used at the beginning of names of people, places, and things. (Page 106)

Character a person or an animal that is in a story. Readers find out about characters by noticing what they say and do. (Page 78)

Compare to tell how things are alike (Page 54)

Conclusion your own idea or opinion about what you read in a passage. Like an inference, a conclusion is based on clues in the reading and what you already know. (Page 46)

Context clues the words and sentences around or near an unknown word that help you figure out what the word means (Page 18)

Contrast to tell how things are different (Page 54)

Fact a statement that is true and can be proved (Page 50)

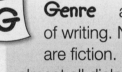

Genre a category, or type, of writing. Novels and stories are fiction. Plays or dramas are almost all dialogue. Nonfiction is based on facts. Poetry has lines and may rhyme. (Page 66)

Graphics tools that help readers better understand information. Charts are one kind of graphic. (Page 14)

Graphic organizers help you arrange and see information in an organized way. Word webs and sequence charts are three examples of graphic organizers. (Page 30)

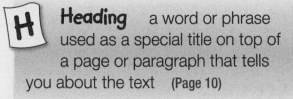

H **Heading** a word or phrase used as a special title on top of a page or paragraph that tells you about the text **(Page 10)**

I **Inference** an educated guess about a passage based on information you read plus information you already know **(Page 42)**

M **Main idea** what a passage is mostly about **(Page 34)**

O **Opinion** a statement that gives someone's feelings or beliefs about something. An opinion cannot be proven. **(Page 50)**

P **Plot** what happens in a story, including all the events from the beginning, middle, and end **(Page 74)**

Punctuation marks within a text that help readers better understand its meaning. A **period** ends a statement. A **question mark** signals a question. An **exclamation point** signals excitement. A **comma** separates cities and states, days and years, and words in a series. **(Page 102)**

Q **Questioning** a way of getting information as you read. Active readers ask themselves "What?" and "Why?" and other questions to better understand the text. **(Page 26)**

R **Reference books** help you find information and answer questions. A **dictionary** tells you what words mean. A **thesaurus** tells you words you can use in place of other words. An **atlas** contains maps. **Encyclopedias** and the **Internet** give information on many topics. (Page 6)

Rhyme the repeating sounds in words at the end of lines in a poem (Page 94)

Rhythm the number of beats or syllables in each line of a poem (Page 94)

S **Sentence** a complete thought. **Declarative sentences** are statements; **imperative sentences** are commands; **interrogative sentences** are questions; and **exclamatory sentences** are exclamations. (Page 98)

Sequence the order in which events happen (Page 58)

Setting where and when a story takes place (Page 82)

Spelling a group of letters that together represent a word. In English, many words follow the same spelling patterns and rules. (Page 110)

 Subject person, place, or thing in a sentence doing an action (Page 114)

Subject-verb agreement whether the subject is singular or plural decides the form of the verb (Page 114)

Summarizing giving the main idea and important details of the text using your own words (Page 90)

Supporting details pieces of information in a passage that support, or tell about, the subject or main idea (Page 38)

T **Text** a piece of published writing used for a purpose. When writing a report, you always want to pick the correct text. (Page 22)

Theme the message or the general meaning of a story (Page 86)

 Verb action word in a sentence (Page 114)

My Words